Contents

This handbook is designed not to be read cover to cover, but for flip through and focus: choose a fault, straight through to a fix...

Contents continued

Contents continued

Contents continued

(The single revolutionary step, which organizers will adopt at
once to fix the problem, and whose effect will be like the way
the Fosbury Flop revolutionized the high jump.)

NOTES ON THE CO-AUTHORS & CO-PIONEERS

There can be few better-qualified than the team of:

John O'Keeffe is a world expert at techniques to achieve high personal performance in the work place (see www.businessbeyondthebox.com). He also reached the British Olympic Squad for hockey, and used these techniques to become a single-figure handicap golfer.

Denis Pugh, who achieved fame as the coach who helped Colin Montgomerie to seven successive European Orders of Merit – eight in all, has coached several successful Ryder Cup players and is expert at communicating techniques as a Sky Sports pundit. He is now interested in helping all golfers getting more out of their technical game, on the course.

Together, they have qualified the **7 Thinking Techniques** by teaching them to over 100 UK PGA professionals and over 1000 golfers of all handicaps.

It's a well-kept secret that, despite the great advance in equipment technology, **average golf scores are no lower.** The two traditional ways to improve are not working:

1 Technical teaching on the range is not enough in itself to significantly lower scores on the course.

2 Looking to Sports Psychology to solve all golf's non-technical problems has been too complicated and impractical for most.

A new, third way is needed to lower golf scores significantly, just like the **Fosbury Flop** revolutionized the high-jump.

...The third, breakthrough way to lower scores is to use the 7 simple thinking techniques that are used successfully on problems outside of golf, and adapt them to your golf.

1 | Introduction
Why NEW GOLF THINKING is needed

For example, the thinking techniques not to **dwell on the failures** you've had on your previous two sales calls today, during the call you are about to make, are similar to what's needed not to still be **thinking of your problems on the first two holes** as you play the par 3 third.

HIGH PERFORMER AT WORK

...BUT AT GOLF

1 | Introduction
Why NEW GOLF THINKING is needed

Similarly, the techniques to **rise to the occasion** when making a speech or presentation, despite being wooden in rehearsal, are similar to what's needed to **do as well, if not better, on the course than you do on the range.**

HIGH PERFORMER AT WORK

Impatient with rehearsal – great on the occasion

...BUT AT GOLF

Fine on the range – can't when it counts

1 | Introduction
Examples of techniques you can learn from outside golf

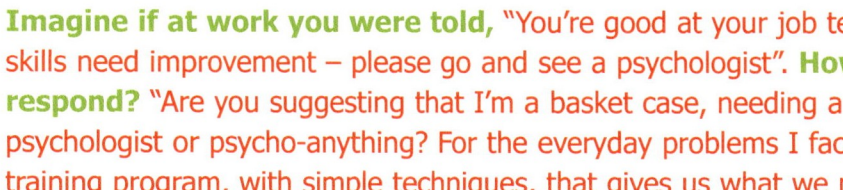

Imagine if at work you were told, "You're good at your job technically, your other skills need improvement – please go and see a psychologist". **How would you respond?** "Are you suggesting that I'm a basket case, needing a psychiatrist, psychologist or psycho-anything? For the everyday problems I face you should have a training program, with simple techniques, that gives us what we need".

But in golf, up to now, for anything non-technical, you have been referred to a psychologist, and many don't want to go. Or, you have to use long, story-telling books or hypnotic CDs, and try to extract practical action to solve everyday problems. That doesn't work for most. Most golfers need simple thinking techniques for the non-technical areas.

Consider two examples:

Example1: Golfers are told to play, "One Shot at a Time". But how do you actually do that? Several tools help. But a key learning from the workplace is **"to measure what you want".** And so, for the first time **NEW GOLF THINKING** does this for golf with the "One Shot at a Time" technique, which follows.

Example 2: Your performance in a round is similar to that in a meeting:
It can get off to a good start or not, can be sticky in the middle, and may or may not have a good finish.
High performers at work learn techniques to hang-on-in-there during a meeting and keep going for the result you want.
That same technique can be used on a golf round, as shown in the "Law of Performance" tool, which also follows.

1 | Introduction
Example 1: THE SHOT PERFORMANCE BULLSEYE

THE SHOT PERFORMANCE BULLSEYE

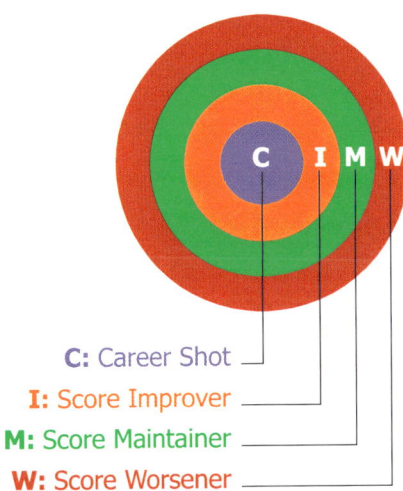

C: Career Shot
I: Score Improver
M: Score Maintainer
W: Score Worsener

How do you play 'One shot at a time' and forget everything else? You cannot put things out of your mind, so instead you have to fill your mind with good things about the shot, such that you don't have room to worry about anything else.

- One start point is to realize that, up to now, there has been no shot-by-shot scoring or measurement system in golf. This contrasts with snooker or pool where you build a long break, but each shot has a measured score. Similarly baseball or cricket, where a long innings is played, each ball has a score and it's then easier to fully focus on doing your very, very best on this shot. For each shot you aim for the very best, perfect execution of what you intend. We'll call this a 'career shot' execution.

- **NEWGOLFTHINKING** now introduces the same for golf, in the form of the **'Shot Performance Bullseye'**

- For each shot you aim for **'Career shot'**. You may not get it, but may hit a **'Score Improver (I)'**; or if not, a **'Score Maintainer (M)'**; or you'll have scored a **'Score Worsener (W)'**.

Examples for the average golfer: (A): Iron shot ends 3ft from flag is an **I**; **(B):** 2nd shot at par 5 mis-hit 150-yards up the middle of the fairway is an **M**; **(C):** Slice into water is a **W**.

You decide what for you is an I, M or W.

Now use a **Practice Scorecard** for a round.

PERFORMANCE ZONE

RESULT

NO RESULT + A STORY

NON-PERFORMANCE ZONE

Story: Greg Louganis the American Olympic gold medalist diver talks about the sweet spot on a diving board. "When you hit it, you zoom up to the perfect position at the top, which makes a great dive easy. Some divers think therefore the secret of top performance is hitting the sweet spot. It's not. That's luck. The secret is what you do when you **don't** hit it...getting to the right place from the wrong place".

- A Universal Law of Performance is that, after a performance, you end up in one of two zones: either with the **result** you wanted or with **no result + a story.**

- Listen to clubhouse conversations. With those who got the result they wanted the conversation is short: "How did you do?" - "Played to my handicap, thanks". With those who didn't: "How did you do?" triggers a long rambling story.

- The key is when you find yourself in the round "concocting in your head" the story you'll tell afterwards" – you have slipped from the **performance zone** to the **non-performance zone**. And you need to flip back to focusing on your result.

- For golf the secret is not to never slip into the **non-performance zone**, it is in realizing when you are beginning to concoct a story, and flipping back to the **performance zone** at once to focus on the **result** you now want.

- Finally note that some people don't have to concoct a story during a round; they bring their story with them to the first tee. They don't even get on to the performance field.

1 | Introduction
The Breakthrough Techniques

HISTORICAL	BREAKTHROUGH
7 technical skills	7 thinking techniques
DRIVING	**BOUNCE-BACK**
IRONS	**RISE-TO-OCCASION**
BUNKER PLAY	**CAN-DO**
PUTTING	**RESULTS-DRIVEN**
CHIPPING	**SELF-START**
OUT-OF-ROUGH	**FRESHEN-UP**
PITCHING	**CLEAR-HEADED**

This chart-book is a breakthrough because, for the first time ever:

- The **non-technical** areas have been simplified to **7 thinking techniques**. These are all you need to solve golf's 'intangibles' – you don't need a brain surgeon nor a degree in psychology.

- A **specific fix** is provided for each of **40 everyday non-technical problems**.

- And each fix is on a simple **chart**, which can be easily reviewed prior to play on a **smart phone** or **tablet**.

This chart-book shows also how a few of the same techniques, and a business-like approach, will **SOLVE SLOW PLAY**. Far more difficult problems than this are solved every day in most organizations.

The '**NEW GOLF THINKING simple system to Solve the Pros' So-Slow Play**'. This is a hugely powerful, practical solution, which the authors expect to be adopted by **all pro tournaments** and sponsors worldwide, with immediate effect.

NEXT STEP: Are you now ready to take on new techniques to lower your scores? Use the 'Push and Pull' technique to increase your intentionality.

1 | **Introduction**
Use Push & Pull

Your **intentionality** to carry something out is a combination of both
The **PULL FORCES...** the pleasure of achieving the goal,
and **PUSH FORCES...** the pain if you stay as you are.
Top performers use both... **goals and goads**
Average performers tend just to use goals... and that's not as powerful.

Pull... A GOAL   **Push... A GOAD**

Pull & Push... GOAL & GOAD

Example: God, to get people to follow the Ten Commandments, used not only gaining the pleasure of Heaven (a big **GOAL**) but also avoiding the pain of Hell (a big **GOAD**)

Example: Top sports people don't just want to win (**GOAL**); they learn to hate to lose (**GOAD**)

The easiest way to "goad" yourself to action is to create in your mind huge dissatisfaction if you don't take action towards result.

Goad yourself to act on the 7 thinking techniques by considering how bad the current system is at achieving lower scores. Goad yourself with the following 5 thoughts.

1 | Introduction
Goad 1: Why do I think the latest gizmo is the solution?

13

31 advances which should have improved scores – but haven't!

RESULT

SAME

- **Go further clubs**
- Go straighter clubs
- **Go further balls, with feel**
- Go further tees
- **Adjustable drivers**
- Bigger sweet-spots
- **Better shafts**
- Better grips for less twist

- **Easy-to- use hybrid clubs**
- Club fitting
- **Better putter faces for smoother rolls**
- Long putters, belly putters
- **Putter fitting**
- Golf-specific physical training
- **Better use of hydration**
- Better use of nourishment
- **Energy saving equipment**
- Better surface fairways

- **Smoother greens**
- Better golf training
- **Sports psychologists**
- Sports psychology books, CDs
- **On-course distance finders**
- Growth in practice ranges
- **Ability to video your swing**
- Ultra-slow-mo of your swing
- **Video side by side swing comparisons**
- TV slow motion analysis of pro swings

- **Multiple YouTube videos of golf instruction**
- Launch monitors to measure: club head speed, ratio of club head speed to ball speed, angle of attack, spin, club path and face angle.
- **Teaching pros to advise on best head type, loft, shaft type, shaft flex, grip type, grip thickness, and best ball type...**

...YET SCORES STAY THE SAME!

1 | Introduction
Goad 2: Why use traditional thinking – when it doesn't work?

TRADITIONAL THINKING	LOWER-SCORE-DRIVEN THINKING
Priority is better full swing	**Priority is on saving shots even with current swing (better putting, chipping, bunkers, distance control with half swing)**
Once the swing is fixed, then for all non-technical problems – go see a psychologist	**No need. Just get good at the 7 Thinking Techniques, whatever your swing, whatever your handicap, whatever your age. These will save you shot after shot**
Endless, aimless, range hitting to swing better, like all others do	**Other sports practice what happens in play. Practice hitting a target, hitting each distance, up and down, one chance**
Teacher doesn't see pupil in competition, and can't direct priorities for lower scores.	**Key is identifying the everyday problems that cause me to lose shots, and putting my available time against fixing them**
Assumption is most improvement comes from a change in hitting	**Easiest improvement, for all levels, comes from a change in thinking**

TRADITIONAL THINKING ISN'T ENOUGH TO LOWER SCORES AND LEAVING SPORTS PSYCHOLOGY TO COVER ALL THE NON-TECHNICAL PROBLEMS DOESN'T WORK

1 | Introduction
Goad 3: Why do I think golf is best taught by psychologists?

The 9 reasons they aren't the (full) answer...

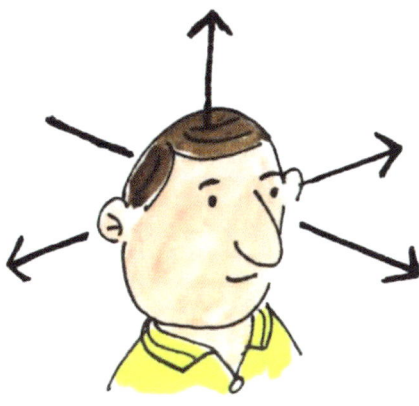

1 NOT ACCESSIBLE: Not enough psychologists anyway to help every golfer.

2 NOT PROVEN: If they were the answer, there would be enough.

3 OFF-PUTTING TITLE: Like psychotherapy, psycho-analysis, psychiatry...thought to be for basket cases.

4 OVER-ENGINEERED: Don't need a brain surgeon for the everyday problems I have on the course; just need the equivalent of a headache pill.

5 ELITE-ORIENTED: Positioned as only for the better player; others wrongly assume they need to fix swing first.

6 FEAR: Going to one may mess with my mind; may ruin what I already have.

7 NOT PRACTICAL: Difficult to put psychology books or CD's into practical action on the course.

8 NO FAULTS AND FIXES: No solution offered for the specific everyday problems of people at my handicap.

9 OVER-COMPLICATED: Much mumbo-jumbo. Shouldn't need a psychology doctorate for my simple problems.

Goad 4: Why do I think TV commentators know best?

The 7 ways they make your scores worse...

1 **They need to make a game that's visually boring, interesting**

Player: needs boringly hit fairways, greens, then sink putts.

2 **They focus on slow-motion swing mechanics to fill in time**

Player: needs no on-course mechanics, more 'bend it like Beckham'.

3 **They exaggerate technical difficulty of shots, to create drama**

Player: needs to get confident over every shot.

4 **They exaggerate the mental pressures on golfers**

Player: needs ways to eliminate pressure, not worsen it.

5 **They make the intangible problems a mysterious part of the game**

Player: needs to see them as simple problems, with simple solutions.

6 **They refer back to the golfers previous difficulties at same shot or hole**

Player: needs to put all that out of their mind.

7 **Suggest no fixes to the intangible issues, since they don't know any**

Player: needs to be reminded of easy fixes to these intangible issues, not treat them as a mystery.

Goad 5: Why do golf authorities not admit current thinking isn't working?

BANKS...

Why did bankers not admit that derivatives and credit default swaps were not fit for purpose?

NEWSPAPERS...

Why did proprietors not admit phone-hacking was widespread and illegal?

UK PARLIAMENT...

Why did MPs not admit that misclaiming on expenses was widespread and illegal?

THE ANSWER...

...IT'S NOT IN THEIR SELF-INTEREST TO ADMIT CURRENT THINKING AND PRACTICE IS WRONG

KEY WAYS THESE 7 THINKING TECHNIQUES ARE VALUABLE TO ALL GOLFERS...

1 They work at every level: these techniques can be used by anyone from a tour professional to a beginner, to dramatically improve their scores.

2 They work at once: unlike a swing-change, which often takes time to work and after which things can be worse for a while, these thinking techniques work at once. Even doing a little bit of just one will help a little bit. The more you do the better you'll score.

3 You can be expert: you can become "the best in the club" at any one of these, with the resultant benefit to your score, no matter how good your swing or how high your handicap. Indeed even as a high handicapper you can get better than many pro golfers at any one of these.

4 They give a faster, easier, bigger benefit: making an improvement in any one of these areas can save you more shots, easier, and quicker, than trying to make an improvement in a technical area e.g. wedge play or driving.

5 Each technique can be learned in under 10-minutes: and there is a visual to help you remember it, or even review it on your Smart Phone or Tablet before you play.

2 The 7 Thinking Techniques
BOUNCE-BACK

HIGH PERFORMER AT WORK

...BUT AT GOLF

**Create response
to handle bad events**

**Trigger negative reactions
to bad events**

2 | The 7 Thinking Techniques
BOUNCE-BACK: How to recover fast from any upset

At work and in life, you encounter obstacles, problems and mini-disasters every day. That's what work and life consists of. It may start with the morning emails, in which some problems arise, and continues through the day...

You quickly learn that if you **get thrown by the first issue**, and start to lose your cool, you find the **next issue more difficult** to handle because you're a bit upset. You learn that things can quickly go from **bad to worse** unless you recover your composure. There are leading edge tools and techniques to help you do this well.

On the golf course, by contrast, we see players not knowing how to **'nip a downward spiral in the bud'**. Something happens to **upset** the player, and as a result the **next shot** is not good, then the **next**. Instead of bouncing-back quickly, things go from bad to worse for a time, and **several shots are wasted**. It happens at every level from high handicapper to the world's best.

The Solution: Use 4 tools which are used to **bounce-back** and achieve breakthrough results in the workplace, and have been adapted to do so on the golf-course. Use them to **bounce-back** quickly from any upset, whether it be a **bad start or a very bad hole**; or things happen that upset you such as your ball landing in an **un-raked bunker, slow play** in front of you, or a **careless noise** just as you're playing. Use them to **avoid things going from bad to worse.**

HIGH PERFORMER AT WORK

...BUT AT GOLF

**Impatient with rehearsal —
great on the occasion**

**Fine on the range —
can't when it counts**

At work and in life, you encounter **many situations in which you want to perform a task well on a particular occasion**: a presentation in a meeting, pitch for new business, a job interview.

You learn to rehearse beforehand, sometimes do dry runs, and then aim be at **your very best 'on the day'.** Often people find they are quite wooden in rehearsal, but they make themselves feel it will come together 'when it's for real'. And there are tools and techniques to help you do this.

By contrast, many **golfers do the opposite**. They find they can hit it **well on the range**, in rehearsal, but don't do as well when it matters and there's a **card in their hand**. And their scores are not as good as they could or should be. They don't **do themselves justice** when it matters.

The Solution: From the Business Beyond the Box program, there are 6 tools that have been adapted to help the golfer **rise-to-the occasion**, rather than crack under pressure: use any of these tools to help you **play well when it matters**; hit your **very best shot more often**, in more circumstances; **keep it going** when you're scoring well; keep your **concentration** up; stop **being inconsistent.**

HIGH PERFORMER AT WORK

...BUT AT GOLF

Chooses powerful
versus
limiting mindsets

Plays in mental bunkers
versus
chooses mental position 'A'

Creates the future

Repeats the past

Can't putt today

By the law of averages, I'll sink the next

Look for ways it can be done

Focuses on ways it can't be done

I'm giving too many shots

He needs the shots because he's so bad

At work and in life, many of your suggestions are often faced initially with a 'can't be done' attitude or response — even when you know it could be done if people put their mind to it.

You have to find a way of **changing their mindset**, or it won't happen. Moreover, when you meet people who have a **limiting mindset** about possibilities for the future, their own situation, or their **likely failure** at something, you sense it's their very **attitude** that holds them back, and you seek to **give them a positive attitude.**

Yet on the golf course, where you don't have anyone to persuade but yourself, many golfers allow themselves to **adopt limiting mindsets** about their own performance e.g. "always mess up this hole", self-sabotage themselves because of that mindset, and after messing up the hole again use it as proof their mindset was right.

The Solution: There are 4 key tools which have been adapted to help golfers stop wasting shots through having limited mindsets.

Use any of these tools to avoid being self-sabotaged by negative mindsets about **certain holes**, shots or situations such as **can't buy a putt** today, can't play in the rain, **always mess-up this hole** or shot, or can't play with a card in my hand. Instead of playing with an inner-voice, which is a negative inner critic, play with an inner-coach who always plays from mental position A.

HIGH PERFORMER AT WORK

Specific, competing goals

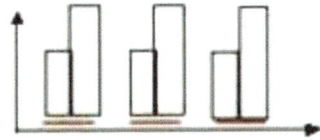

Plan, progress, fulfilment

Building steps to goal

DRIVEN: "We will find
a way or we will make one"

...BUT AT GOLF

Pastime, goal-less

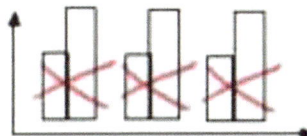

Mystery, frustration, dissatisfaction

Endless tip-searching

DRIFTING: Amongst a sea
of vague wishes

2 | The 7 Thinking Techniques
RESULTS-DRIVEN: How to sort out exactly what you want

There are two parts to this technique: (A) the focus on results; and (B) being driven to achieve them.

Consider: Focus on results:

At work and in life, you learn to work towards clear goals, and the priorities between several goals e.g. do you want to maximize sales or maximize profit or a balance between the two.

In life, you learn to **trade-off** some spending now, to be able to afford something later you want more.

By contrast many golfers haven't worked out what they **really want**, what trade-offs to accept, and so often end up **frustrated**. It is like fishing: many people go fishing, **but don't realize it's not the fish they are after**. So with golf, many players haven't sorted out in their minds what result they want between **having fun, hitting it better or further, and scoring well**. Moreover, they change priorities depending on mood; e.g. the round isn't going well, so switch to having fun.

Much current golf teaching is not **result-focused, it's swing focused**. Almost uniquely in sports coaching, your teacher doesn't watch you perform to get your score, doesn't know what you scored and **why you scored it**. The **hidden assumption** is that the way **to score better on the course is to try and swing better on the range.** This has proven to be a **MYTH**. At best, it's not the top priority for reducing your scores, yet golfers and their teachers spend all their time on it. You wouldn't do that in business, or in life.

At work and in life you know how important to success determination is...

In golf, people say they want a better score, but often are **not prepared to do much** to get it. It's fine if they find a new tip or technique to try, but even then aren't prepared to **persevere or practice**, and quickly move on in the search for the **next magic instant cure.**

Most golfers are not fully **results-driven**: yes they want a lower score, but put obstacles in the way in terms of what they are not prepared to do achieve it, e.g. want to carry on using the same old putter I've always used.

The Solution: There are 5 breakthrough tools which help business people become more '**driven**'. These are easily adapted to be used in golf, by anyone from a tour professional to a beginner:

Use these tools to build your **determination** to do what it takes to lower your scores; **to hang on in there** in a round, to **do yourself justice**; and to hit shots with **conviction rather than hope**.

HIGH PERFORMER AT WORK

Play inside-out

...BUT AT GOLF

Play outside-in

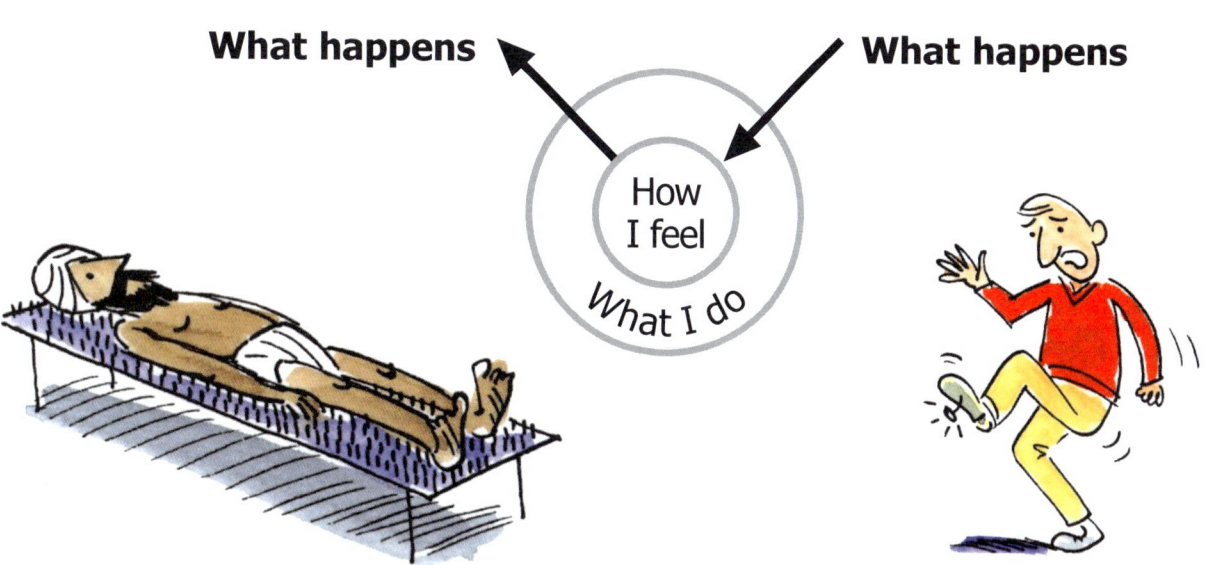

What happens

What happens

How
I feel

What I do

I happen to the world

The world happens to me

He or she shows **confidence** in solving the problem, and that confidence is so strong it runs off on others. And while some run around like headless chickens, he gets the group **focused** on what needs to be done. He is not only able to **self-start** himself **calm, confident and focused**, he does it so well he gets others to the same states.

By contrast, **on the golf course**, many people **start off unconfident** and need to wait until and if something good **happens to give themselves confidence**. They are anxious, until and if something happens to calm their nerves. And whilst they wait, they don't play at their best. They have to **wait for a putt to drop before** they can putt confidently, rather than get confident and that gets the putt.

The Solution: Use new tools to **self-start** yourself into the state you wish play in. Use these tools to get yourself **out of unproductive moods** on the course; to **stop** the occasions of **tense and anxious, or frustrated**; and instead make yourself calm, confident and focused, and well able to **handle pressure**.

At work, **a big problem** may arise which people may be **anxious and unconfident** about solving. They may even begin to panic. **A leader** learns to be **calm himself** in this situation, to exude calm, and through that to calm others.

2 | The 7 Thinking Techniques
FRESHEN-UP: GET FRESH versus STAY HEAVY

This skill will illustrate two opposite feelings:

- **At work**, after two unproductive sales calls, he **freshens up** and makes the next call the best of the month.

- **In golf**, after starting with two bad holes, he **feels like giving up the game**, and doesn't realize the next hole is a hole-in-one opportunity.

At work, you have to find ways to be at your very best for your eleven o'clock meeting, even though your nine o'clock meeting was a disaster.

The only way a salesperson can succeed is to have a fresh attitude for the next call even if all the previous calls have failed. A teacher **has to be fresh** to teach the coming class well, even though a **previous class didn't go well.**

By contrast, many a **golfer playing the 14th hole** still seems to have a heavy heart because of the short putt they **missed badly on the 8th**, or even something that **happened on the 2nd!** And because he still has something **weighing on his mind**, he's not at his best, and doesn't play at his best.

The Solution: learn to use the three key tools for golf, which help you put things behind you in life and the workplace.

Use these tools to **stop previous bad shots** or bad holes **weighing on your mind**; to stop past mistakes or incidents in the round **affecting you now**; and instead get that **'fresh-start'** feeling on every tee or shot, not just on the 10th tee.

2 | The 7 Thinking Techniques
CLEAR-HEADED

AT WORK: Ask for enough budget

AT GOLF: Take too little club

AT WORK: Avoid predicatable trouble

AT GOLF: Court disaster

AT WORK: Time with prime prospects

AT GOLF: Time spent mindlessly
on range

PRACTICE TIME

	Score Improvement potential %	Current %	Planned %
Driving	_____	_____	_____
Iron Play	_____	_____	_____
Chipping/Pitching	_____	_____	_____
Putting	_____	_____	_____
Non-Technical	_____	_____	_____
	100	100	100

At work people expect themselves to be clear-headed. For example, you learn to prioritize your time to get the best results, by focusing on the biggest sales opportunities.

Yet **golfers** who know the easiest way to lower their score is by **spending time practicing putting**, chipping, or shots under 100-yards still spend most of their time on the **full swing on the range**.

At work, people take action to **avoid predictable trouble**. At golf, people know all the trouble is at the **front of the green**, but never play to the back.

At work, people make sure their **budget for a job has some slack** for contingencies. At golf, the attitude is **"I shouldn't need more than an 8-iron** for that distance", and will continue to use the skeleton inadequate budget of an 8-iron, even when time after time they are short.

The Solution: Use specific thinking tools and techniques to get **clear-headed** about your golf, and about your approach to practice to lower your score.

THE ISSUE: In what business or organization would you tolerate a problem that spoils the enjoyment of all; is getting worse; threatens the future of the enterprise; a problem everyone wants to solve.

Yet the authorities, committees and leading figures talk about it but don't fix it ...and remain in position to talk about it and not fix it next year either. Yet the problem is far easier to solve than many problems people solve at work.

CURRENT SLOW PLAY EFFORTS: Are weak in a business-like approach in 3 of the 7 Thinking Techniques:

Weak in RESULTS-DRIVEN: Not even focused on the result that's sought: Duration of Round - (DOR) is not measured, recorded, nor communicated. There is no drive to improve it: neither a compelling goal, nor a meaningful goad e.g. no bad consequence for slow play.

Weak in CAN-DO: Golfers feel they are helpless victims of the problem; feel that it is up to others to implement the same-old solutions, and it's because they don't do this that the problem persists. No-one takes responsibility for solving it.

Weak in CLEAR-HEADED: Committees feel they've done their job if they re-issue guidelines and target times, even if that action isn't solving the problem. No smart action of what to be fixed by whom by when, with a consequence if it doesn't happen.

SOLUTION: Go to Chapter 11

3 | BOUNCE-BACK
How to stop getting upset by things that happen

THE FIRST LAW OF RESILIENCE...

 + =

Question: "What has to be added to any event to make it into a problem?"

Answer ....

- **Example:** The event is: a huge **'BANG'** nearby.

  Problem? If interpreted as explosion ...yes

  If interpreted as car back-firing ...no

- **The First Law of Resilience is:**
  EVENT + **'INTERPRETATION'** = **PROBLEM**

- Our first instinct, due to our survival instinct, is to see how any event could be a potential problem for us. So we interpret the event as a problem and become upset.

- However, we can always choose an **alternative interpretation**. It's our choice.

  Story: Two shoe salesmen came down the plane steps to a new country: "There's no opportunity", said one, "they don't wear shoes"; "There's a huge opportunity", said the other," they don't wear shoes".

- Instead of seeing the event as a problem, and being upset by it, how could you interpret it as an opportunity, a challenge or an adventure, and be excited by it?

3 | BOUNCE-BACK
How to stop things going from bad to worse

SPIRAL UP versus SPIRAL DOWN

Consider, as an example from life, a sudden unexpected, big, traffic jam on the way to work...

- **Spend a full 3-minutes now to write down all the reasons and ways this may be a problem to you.** What are the potential bad consequences for you? And what are the possible bad consequences of those consequences? Do spend 3-minutes doing this exercise, imagining the worst possible consequences.
  Note them down ....
  ....
  ....

- The more you think about the possible sequences, the more of a **PROBLEM** it is! Look again, traffic still hasn't moved ... now even **BIGGER PROBLEM**. You react against it, tap wheel, sound horn, shout etc. This is the **DOWNWARD REACTIVE SPIRAL**.

- Once you are wound up about the traffic jam, the next thing to happen to you in the day is likely to seem a problem, too. One thing after the other, it goes from bad to worse. You get tighter and tighter.

...This is 'SPIRALLING DOWN'

SPIRAL UP versus SPIRAL DOWN...

An **alternative interpretation** is always possible...

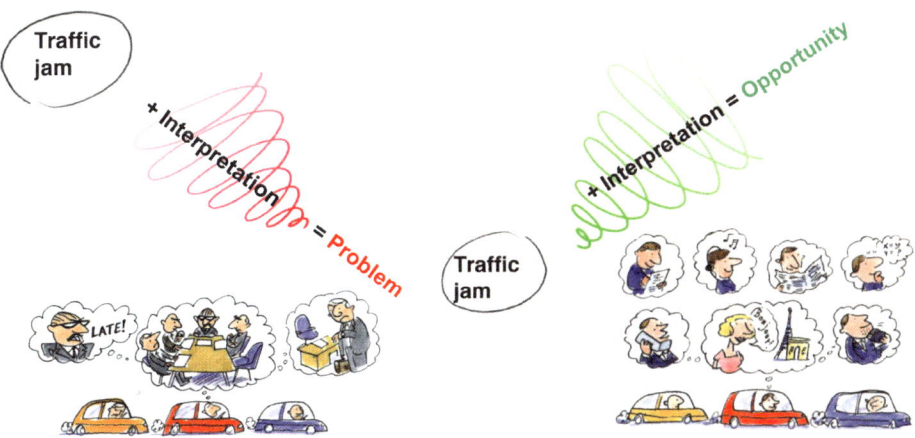

How might the traffic jam be an 'OPPORTUNITY?' What sort of things might you do in a traffic jam?

Note these down now. Everything that comes to mind. Spend 3 minutes on this. Get more and more creative as you think. The answers don't have to be logically correct. Funny or ridiculous is fine. As you get more and more creative you get lighter and lighter.

....

....

....

....

This is the UPWARD CREATIVE SPIRAL...

...This is 'SPIRALLING UP'

3 | BOUNCE-BACK
How to stop things going from bad to worse

SPIRAL UP versus SPIRAL DOWN...

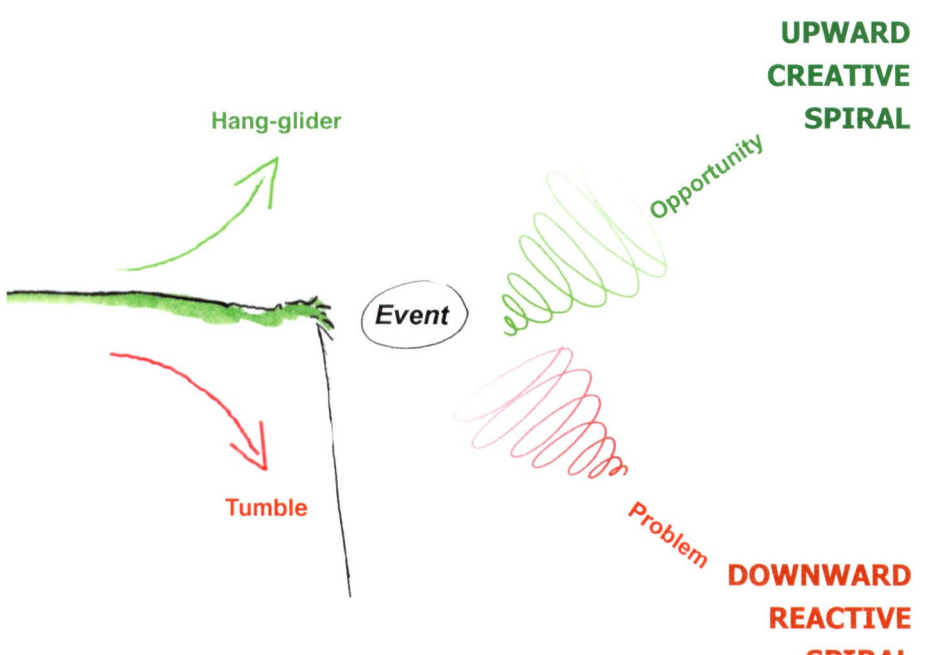

UPWARD CREATIVE SPIRAL

Hang-glider

Opportunity

Event

Tumble

Problem

DOWNWARD REACTIVE SPIRAL

So here are two alternative spirals of thought:

- the **DOWNWARD, REACTIVE, PROBLEM** spiral, where you get tighter and tighter and the event is above you

- the **UPWARD, CREATIVE OPPORTUNITY** spiral, where you get lighter and lighter and you are above the event

It's like going off the edge of a cliff:

- you can **tumble** down the reactive problem spiral

- You can take a **hang-glider** and soar up above the event

3 | BOUNCE-BACK
How to stop things going from bad to worse

This is your RESPONSE-ABILITY

DOWNWARD SPIRAL

EVENT   **REACTION**

REA**C**TIVE

UPWARD SPIRAL

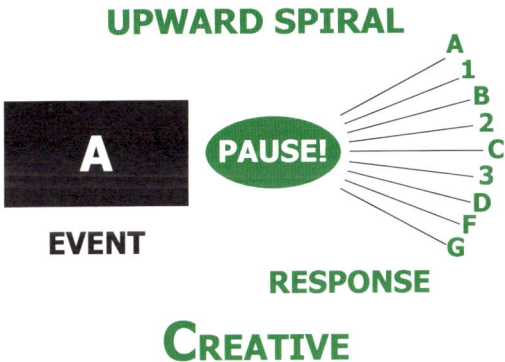

EVENT

RESPONSE

CREATIVE

- The downward spiral is where you **REACT** to the event. The event is A. What follows A? **B**.

- The upward spiral is where you **PAUSE** after the event and then choose a **RESPONSE**.

- The event is **A**. **PAUSE**. What else might follow A?

  How might **A** follow A rather than **B**? What might **AA** stand for?...........

  How might **C** follow A rather than **B**? What might **AC** stand for?...........

  How might **D** follow A rather than **B**? What might **AD** stand for?..........

  How might **1** follow A rather than **B**? What might **A1** stand for? ....

It does not have to be **B** after **A**. You can choose to respond with **A, C or anything.**

- One spiral is **REACTIVE**. The other **CREATIVE**. The difference is your **RESPONSE-ABILITY**

- What is the only spelling difference between **REA**C**TIVE** and **C**REATIVE**?.............

..The DIFFERENCE is **HOW YOU 'C' IT**

3 | BOUNCE-BACK
Stop being put off by the same, predictable things

TRAFFIC LIGHTS

Traffic lights are put at predictable danger spots:

- When you are on **amber** there are two alternatives, you next see **red — reactive** ...or you next see **green — creative**

- You can **PREDICT** what may be the 'traffic lights on amber' situations for you on the course, where you are in danger of going **red**, e.g. landing in **unraked bunker**

- So you can **PLAN** in advance, for each possible **amber** situation, how not to see **red (reactive)**, but to create interpretations to continue unfazed on **green (creative)**.

TOOL SHEET: Predict traffic light junctions. How might you interpret the following events as opportunities?

POSSIBLE EVENT	CREATE WAYS TO SEE THE EVENT AS AN OPPORTUNITY
Mis-hit shot	....
Ball plugged in bunker	....
Bad tee shot on 1st tee	....
Slow play in front	....
Ball lands close from behind	....
Ball in divot on fairway	....
Noise on backswing	....
Putt hits spike mark	....
Unfair pin position	....
Ball in unraked bunker spot	....
Bad weather	....
Long wait on tee	....
Long wait between shots	....
Stupid remarks by playing partner	....
Partners don't look for your ball	....
Bad play by playing partners	....
Miss a very short putt	....
Don't get out of bunker	....
Poor etiquette by others	....
Talk during your swing	....
Unexpectedly lost ball	....
Do a hook/slice/top	....

3 BOUNCE-BACK

Stop being put off by the same, predictable things

TOOL SHEET: Predict traffic light junctions...

My top 10 worst events

Create ways to see 'GREEN'

....

....

....

....

....

....

....

....

....

....

....

3 | BOUNCE-BACK
How to stop messing it up when in trouble

Some events in golf, however, cannot be predicted. You don't know in advance where the amber warning signal will be.

Assume a totally unexpected event happens, which gives you a 'PROBLEM', or puts you into 'TROUBLE' Remember there's a **"whole worLd behind every word"**. Each word has its own website of meaning

- **If you consider it as 'trouble', the only way your brain can understand what you mean is to visit your personal website for "trouble" and find what is on it in terms of your life experience and associated feelings, e.g. illness, house burning down, being in bad debt, trouble with the police. You access those nerve endings.**

- So write down as per the next chart, all the things/feelings/consequences that come to mind if you say **"this is trouble"**, **e.g. bad consequences, problem, worry, failure.** What state does **www.trouble** leave you in? At precisely the moment you need to be resourceful, you visit the most unhelpful website, and you perform badly.

- Now what things come to mind when you visit **www.adventure**? Write these down, **e.g. fun, challenge, excited**.

- Whatever now happens on the golf course, consider it as AN ADVENTURE, and access those helpful feelings

"TROUBLE becomes ADVENTURE"

3 BOUNCE-BACK
How to stop messing it up when in trouble

TOOL SHEET: www.adventure versus **www.trouble**

www.trouble... **TROUBLE** conjures up for me:

....
....
....
....
....
....
....
....
....
....
....
....
....

www.adventure... **ADVENTURE** conjures up for me:

....
....
....
....
....
....
....
....
....
....
....
....
....

RELIEVE PRESSURE – THRIVE ON THRILL

Putting yourself under **PRESSURE**

Giving yourself a **THRILL**

- Feeling you are playing **'UNDER PRESSURE'** blocks performance. But a feeling, which is very close to pressure, but is very different, is **THRILL**. Seeing it **'AS A THRILL'** to play in this situation, boosts performance.

- So how do you get from **'PRESSURE'** to **'THRILL'** ?

- **Exercise:**
  - 7 ft curly downhill putt to win The Open. Pressure? Yes.
    If you're not fully confident and feel big consequences if you miss.

  - 7 inch putt to win The Open. Pressure? No.
    Because fully confident of success.

  - 7 ft curly downhill putt to win a friendly rollup match. Pressure? No.
    Because it would be a THRILL to get it and no big bad consequences if you miss.

PRESSURE comes from low confidence of success, and imagining big bad consequences if you miss.

THRILL comes from **high confidence** of success, and thinking there are **no big bad consequences** if you miss.

RELIEVE PRESSURE – THRIVE ON THRILL

www.PRESSURE

www.THRILL

MAKE **BIG** IN YOUR MIND:..

CONSEQUENCES of **FAILING!**

CONFIDENCE of doing it!

BENEFITS of succeeding!

Make small in your mind...

Confidence of doing it; Benefits of succeeding

Consequences of failing

It's **CHOICE** not **CHANCE** whether you experience
PRESSURE or **THRILL**

- You can decide what to "blow up out of proportion" in your mind, and what to "make light of".

- This is your Inner Kingdom, you are the Ruler

- To get to **THRILL:**
  - Blow up your **CONFIDENCE** of doing it
  - Play up the **BENEFITS** of doing it
  - Play down the consequences of missing

- How could you do this?
  Use attached tool sheet.

TOOL SHEET: RELIEVE PRESSURE – THRIVE ON THRILL

1 The things I can choose to recall vividly that will make me **CONFIDENT** of doing this: e.g. go to mental scrapbook (see later) focus on previous successful experiences; change body, words; if missed before, use the law of averages; recall practice; recall learnings; imagine the practice ground.

2 The pleasurable thrill I can imagine from doing this, the **BENEFITS** I'll get:

3 The things I can say to myself as to why it's not a big **CONSEQUENCE** if I fail: e.g. "Compared to a relative's illness, the consequences of missing this putt are low. But it would be a thrill to get it, and I can". e.g. Pre-putt routine: "By the time I've walked all the way round the putt, 2 people will have died of AIDS in Africa. Compared to that, the consequences of missing this are very small".

THE SHOT PERFORMANCE BULLSEYE

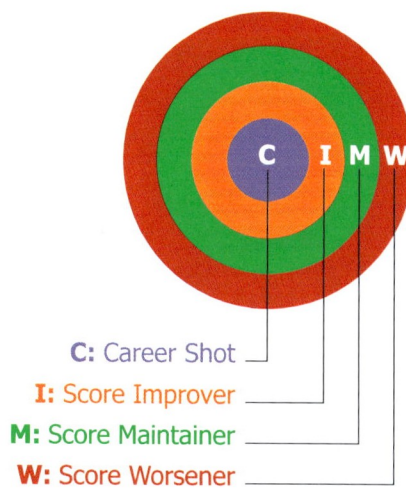

C: Career Shot
I: Score Improver
M: Score Maintainer
W: Score Worsener

How do you play "One shot at a time" and forget everything else? You cannot put things out of your mind, so instead you have to fill your mind with good thoughts that help focus on the shot, such that you don't have room to worry about anything else.

- The start point is to realize that, up to now, there has been no shot-by-shot scoring or measurement system in golf. This contrasts with snooker or pool where you build a long break, but each shot has a measured score. Similarly baseball or cricket, where a long innings is played, each ball has a score and it's then easier to fully focus on doing your very best on this current shot.

- **NEWGOLFTHINKING** now introduces a similar meaurement system for golf, in the form of the **'Shot Performance Bullseye'.** For each shot you aim for the very best, perfect execution of what you intend. We'll call this a **'Career Shot'** execution.

- You may not get it, but may hit a **'Score Improver (I)'**; or if not, a **'Score Maintainer (M)'**; or you'll have scored a **'Score Worsener (W)'**.

Examples for the average golfer: (A): Iron shot ends 3ft from flag is an **I**; **(B):** 2nd shot at par 5 mis-hit 150-yards up the middle of the fairway is an **M**; **(C):** Slice into water is a **W**.

You decide what for you is an I, M or W.

Now use the attached **Practice Scorecard** for a round.

4 Rise-to-occasion
Play 'one shot at a time' – PRACTICE SCORECARD

For each shot & putt, prepare to hit a 'C'. Then **mark down**, after the shot, whether it was a **C**, **I**, **M** or **W**. Then, on the next shot, again aim for a 'C' execution, & mark down the result. Practice until you do this on every single shot for a round. You will then be playing 'one shot at a time'.

Next, overleaf, learn to play 'your **BEST** shot, time after time'.

	PAR	SCORE	TEE SHOT	2ND	3RD	4TH	5TH	6TH	7TH	TOTAL:	I	M	W
1													
2													
3													
4													
5													
6													
7													
8													
9													
OUT													
10													
11													
12													
13													
14													
15													
16													
17													
18													
IN													
TOTAL													

MENTAL LIBRARY OF 3D CAREER SHOTS

SHOT	COURSE/HOLE	SHOT	COURSE/HOLE
Drive		6 Iron	
3 Wood		7 Iron	
Hybrid		8 Iron	
3 Iron		9 Iron	
4 Iron		Full PW	
5 Iron		1/2 PW	

To produce the best you can, you need to recall, or imagine, the best you can. To play a career-best 7-iron, you need to recall the best 7-iron you have hit, or can hit.

- Make a table like the attached to note down the course/hole of the best shot you can remember hitting with each club. It could be that the course you were on was 'the range'. Extend the table to include all your clubs, and half swings with your wedges and chips, bunker shots and putts. Better players can include variants, e.g. best drawn 3-wood, best faded 3-wood.

- The issue now is ... how to produce this **career shot time after time**, or at least as close to it as you can?

- You do it through the 3 steps of the **RAF: Mental Shot Routine...**

1 **R**EHEARSE in 3D

2 **A**IM to bulls-eye through needle eye

3 **F**LOW

RAF MENTAL SHOT ROUTINE:

1 REHEARSE in 3D

Spider phobia

Public speaking

Dream

TRIGGER

A pattern of:
- **Muscle memory**
- **Nervous impulses**

- The first step is to **FULLY REHEARSE** the shot in your mind in 3 dimensions – **vividly feel it, see it, hear it.** This is significantly more helpful than traditional thinking. Most golfers will say they 'visualize' the shot — but how vividly? And 'seeing' it anyway is not enough. Your best shot will come from a 'Full Dress Rehearsal' in your mind — the sight, the sound, the feel.

- By imagining something vividly this way we can access **muscle memory and nervous impulses**. Some people just need to think of a spider and their body shivers with fright. The mere thought of public speaking can cause a cold sweat. Just thinking of certain people touching you can cause you to wince. A vivid dream will similarly access muscle memories and nervous impulses 'as though it were real'.

- The more we can imagine the career shot **'very vividly'** the more the effect on our body. It's not just 'lip-service visualization', it's 'living the shot'.

- The way we imagine something vividly, is to **'Live it in 3D'**. The 3 dimensions are... **FEEL it, HEAR it, SEE it.**

The more we do all 3, the more we live the shot, the bigger the effect on the body. ▶

4 | Rise-to-occasion
How to play your best shot, time after time

RAF MENTAL SHOT ROUTINE:

1 REHEARSE in 3D

Test each 'D"

How do you tie shoelaces?

What's the 4th letter of the alphabet?

What's the colour of your front door?

Maximise a memory

FEEL it in every fibre

HEAR every little sound

SEE it in graphic detail

Test for yourself how each of feel, hear, and see accesses a different part of the brain, using the examples:

• Prepare for a moment to write down how you tie shoelaces. Think about it for a minute. The only way to explain it is to first 'feel' yourself actually doing it in your mind. That's the **FEEL** part of your brain.

• Most people find out the fourth letter after D by reciting the alphabet to yourself in your mind… That's the **HEAR** part of your brain.

• You check the colour of your front door by **SEEING** it in your brain.

Note: to maximize a memory you do all three of 3D, each one in the most intense detail you can. ▶

4 | Rise-to-occasion
How to play your best shot, time after time

RAF MENTAL SHOT ROUTINE:

1 REHEARSE in 3D

3D car buying

3D love

Test for yourself the importance of each of the 3D's, and why all 3 together have best effect.

- **Car buying:** Salesman only shows you it **(SEE)**. Not enough, you want to drive it for yourself **(FEEL)**.
  Salesman only lets you drive it **(FEEL)**. Not enough, you want to hear the history **(HEAR)**.

He'll likely only make a sale if he lets you **HEAR** its history, lets you **SEE** it, lets you drive **(FEEL)** it.

- **Love strategy:** "I love you" he says, "No you don't" she says
  "I'm always telling you I do" **(HEAR)**, "But you don't show me **(SEE)** any more" e.g. with presents
  "I'm always cuddling you" **(FEEL)**, "I wish you'd stop mauling me and talk" **(HEAR)**

One alone is insufficient. When you are "courting" you use all three: whisper sweet nothings **(HEAR)**; give presents **(SEE)** and kisses and cuddles **(FEEL)**.

For best results, you need to similarly **SEE, FEEL,** and **HEAR** your career shot

Next, what to think about as you prepare to play your career shot? Don't think of a **PINK ELEPHANT.** ▶

4 | Rise-to-occasion
How to play your best shot, time after time

RAF MENTAL SHOT ROUTINE:

1 REHEARSE in 3D

"DON'T SPILL THE DRINK!"

You thought of a pink elephant. The mind cannot visualize **'not'**. So to not think of a pink elephant the mind at once visualizes a pink elephant.

• Remember the more urgent/important things are, the more you access the muscle memory. **"Don't spill the drink!"** particularly on an expensive carpet, accesses the muscle memory and nervous system for spilling drink. **"Don't touch the hot plate!"** produces the same effect. You need instead to focus on accessing what you do want to do, i.e., **"Hold it steady, you can do it"** instead of **"Don't spill the drink!"**

• Translate this learning to your golf shot: **"Must not slice into the water on the right"** accesses the muscle memory to do precisely that. The more important/tense the situation, the more the access. Sometimes good players will realize at the last minute they have accessed the wrong muscle memory, and will over compensate with a huge pull left.

Instead of **thinking what to avoid**, instead **focus on hitting your career shot**. How? ▶

RAF MENTAL SHOT ROUTINE:

1 REHEARSE in 3D

GOOD FOCUS		BAD FOCUS
WHAT YOU WANT	versus	**WHAT YOU DON'T WANT**
DREAM PRECISELY	versus	**DREAM VAGUELY**
DREAD VAGUELY		**DREAD PRECISELY**

Now consider the mental library worksheet overleaf...

• Consider your **career shots**. Imagine now the situation. Prepare to **SEE**, **FEEL** and **HEAR**, vividly.

1. SEE: Remember the shot and hole in vivid colour. How did the ball flight go, exactly? Straight,...or draw? How much? How high did it rise above the background? How did it land, and roll? Can you see it all very clearly? Then tick the **SEE** box.

2. FEEL: Can you now "feel" that shot vividly in your mind? Feel the club, your body, your swing, your finish etc? Tick the **FEEL** box.

3. HEAR: Now can you "hear" the sounds associated with your career shot? Perhaps the sound of the strike...it's amazing how you can recognize a good strike, putt or chip just by its sound. Can you hear what anyone said about the career shot? Tick the **HEAR** box. Make sure you can **SEE**, **FEEL** and **HEAR** the career shot you've chosen. The more detail the better.

That's 'Rehearsal in 3D' — the first part of the RAF shot routine.

Next you need to transpose it to **this** hole... **This is the second part of the RAF shot routine.**

A NEW GOLF THINKING TOOL SHEET: Mental library of career shots

SHOT	COURSE HOLE	VIVID SEE	VIVID HEAR	VIVID FEEL	3D REHEARSAL
Drive					
3 Wood					
3 Hybrid					
4 Hybrid					
5 Hybrid					
4 Iron					
5 Iron					
6 Iron					
7 Iron					
8 Iron					
9 Iron					
Full PW					
1/2 PW					
3/4 PW					
SW					
Long Bunker					
Short Bunker					
Long Chip					
Medium Chip					
Long Putt					
Medium Putt					
Short Putt					
Downhill Putt					
Uphill Putt					

RAF MENTAL SHOT ROUTINE:

2 AIM to BULLSEYE through NEEDLE-EYE

Where do you aim?

FAT, WEAK AIM	BULLSEYE AIM
Out of bunker	
On fairway	
On green	
Chip close	
Lag up	
On green at Par 3	
'Approach' shot	

Q: Where do you aim in archery?

Answer...
....

And why do you aim there?

Answer...
....

There are three reasons:

The first is that hitting the bull gets you the best score. Second, if you aim for the bull and miss, you'll be closer than if you just aim for the outer circle.

• So get an absolute, detailed, specific bulls eye for each shot.

• By contrast, golf terminology is full of **'fat, weak aims'**. For each of the fat aims shown, substitute an aim which is the equivalent of **'the bullseye'.** ▶

RAF MENTAL SHOT ROUTINE:

2 AIM to BULLSEYE through NEEDLE-EYE

The third reason for a detailed aim is the 'thread the needle eye effect'.

• Can you carry on an argument while closing a drawer? Yes.

• Can you carry on an argument whilst threading a needle? No.

Threading a needle takes all your concentration. It absorbs all your mental attention... and you cannot be thinking about the double bogey on last hole, your bad sand shot, whatever.

• So now plan to hit your career shot here and now **'to a bulls eye through a needle eye'**, e.g. for 5-iron in reach of the green.

• Recall vividly your career 5-iron. See it, feel it, hear it in your mind

• Aim now to hole it (bullseye)

• What needle eye path will it take?

• Pick a tree on the horizon it will be in line with. Which branch? Exactly. Decide!

• How much above the tree line will it rise?

• Will it be straight? Or fade ... how much?

• Where will it land? See it roll into the hole.

That's 'To Bullseye through Needle Eye', the second step of the Mental shot routine.

RAF MENTAL SHOT ROUTINE:

3 F LOW

GO WITH FLOW...

...STOP WITH HOW

Now 'GO WITH FLOW' ...just let it go.

- Consider the many **difficult** things your body can do if you **'just do it'**. See the examples above.

- Consider how each of them becomes more difficult, not easier, if you stop to think how to do it.

- **Example:**
  - Walk along a plank on the ground – **easy, just do it.**

  - Put plank in air between two buildings – **can't do it, if you start thinking,** "how should feet be, how fast/slow, where should arms be, where to face, etc". That **stops** you. Only way is to 'just do it'.

- Best worldwide example: David Beckham free kicks. Do you analyze them like golf swings? No, practice... then just do it – **'Bend it like Beckham'.**

RAF MENTAL SHOT ROUTINE:

PUTTING RAF TOGETHER

GO WITH FLOW

STOP WITH HOW

R **Rehearse:** your career shot in 3D – **FEEL it, HEAR it, SEE it.**

A **Aim:** Step up to the address position. Imagine putting your feet into the spotlight, the performance circle. You **AIM** it… **to a Bullseye through a Needle Eye.**

F **'GO WITH FLOW'…** just let it go 'just do it'.

Now use the **Shot Routine Scorecard** attached in a practice round to develop the right habits.

For each shot aim to do all three parts of the mental pre-shot routine.

R **3D rehearsal of career shot FEEL HEAR SEE**

A **Bullseye through Needle Eye**

F **GO WITH FLOW**

For each shot, afterwards mark with a tick whether you've done each of these three well.

PRACTICE SCORECARD: check full RAF shot routine on each shot

	PAR	SCORE	TEE SHOT			2nd			3rd			4th			5th			6th			7th			TOTAL		
			R	A	F	R	A	F	R	A	F	R	A	F	R	A	F	R	A	F	R	A	F	R	A	F
1																											
2																											
3																											
4																											
5																											
6																											
7																											
8																											
9																											
OUT																											
10																											
11																											
12																											
13																											
14																											
15																											
16																											
17																											
18																											
IN																											
TOTAL																											

PUTTING IT ALL TOGETHER IN COMPETITION

	Tee Shot	2ND	3RD	4TH	5TH	6TH	7TH	TOTAL I's	PAR	SCORE
	–	5						1		
	D						P	2		
TOTAL										

- Use the **Competition Scorecard** overleaf when competing. But only mark down **Score Improvers**... because in competition you want to remind yourself of the **great** shots

- Aim on each shot to hit a **'career shot'**.

- Do the **RAF shot routine: FEEL it, HEAR it, SEE it; To Bullseye through Needle Eye; GO WITH FLOW.**

- If you then achieve at least a score improver, mark it down. As shown on this card:

  - on the first hole the second shot, a 5-iron was a score improver

  - on the second, the drive was, and a putt was

  ...now you are on the 3rd tee – aim for a career shot with **this** shot

ACHIEVING YOUR BEST SHOT IN COMPETITION

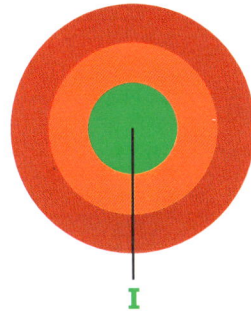

I

1 Aim for a 'C'

2 Do full RAF

3 Note 'I' & 'C'

	Tee Shot	2ND	3RD	4TH	5TH	6TH	7TH	TOTAL I's	PAR	SCORE
TOTAL										

HOW YOUR MINDSET DRIVES YOUR ACTION

SPOT A MIND SET

The sand is too little/deep/soft...

The greens are too fast/slow/bumpy...

I always mess up this hole...

Lessons don't work for me...

What others do you hear?

....

....

....

....

....

- A mindset is a bias, a prejudice or an attitude. It can arise from repeatedly telling yourself something. It becomes a personal internal 'rule', which you think is right.

- Mindsets are key because nowadays we don't have time to think everything through from first principles. We operate according to our internal rules.

- It is our **mindset** which dictates three things:

what we do,

what we don't do,

what we let happen.

YOUR MINDSET DRIVES:

• **what you DO** • **what you do NOT DO** • **what you LET HAPPEN**

Too many cooks spoil the broth

Can't teach an old dog new tricks

Place on course is just ahead of group behind

Many hands make light work

Never too late to learn

Place on course is just behind group in front

• Compare the alternative mindsets on this chart. If someone thinks **"Too many cooks spoil the broth"...** the things he/she will do in a situation, and not do, and let happen ... will be the opposite of someone who thinks **"Many hands make light work"**.

• If the mindset of every fourball is **"Our place on the course is just behind the group in front"**, what they will **DO** (e.g. walk briskly between shots to catch up), **NOT DO** (e.g. mark cards on the green) **AND LET HAPPEN** (e.g. if someone ready let them play even out of turn) will be different to groups who think **"Our place is just ahead of the group behind".** And because of their mindset, the first set of fourballs would be quicker

**...Your choice of mindset will dictate your results,
it is a Self–Fulfilling Circle.**

5 | CAN-DO:
How to stop self-sabotage from negative mindsets

THE SELF-FULFILLING CIRCLE

Key Learning: The circle can be:
-ve or **+ve** – it works both ways.

-ve thoughts > **-ve** mindset >
-ve action > **-ve** results *or...*
+ve thoughts > **+ve** mindset >
+ve action > **+ve** results

4
RESULTS

3
ACTION

1
MINDSET

**GETS
CEMENTED**

2

Let's go round the SELF-FULFILLING CIRCLE

1 MINDSET: (a) The more we repeat thoughts to ourselves, the more they become a mindset (say something often enough to yourself and you start to believe it); **(b)** The more important or pressured the situation, the more our mindset dictates our behaviour because we don't have time to think things through.

2 GETS CEMENTED: Once we have a mindset, it gets easily cemented. We all want to be right about ourselves (way back when our very survival depended on being right). We all therefore cherry-pick data to show our mindset is right. Why do people believe in horoscopes? Because they unknowingly cherry-pick data that supports what the horoscope said. Why do some people think that some pet-owners look like their pets? Because with that mindset, they cherry-pick the two or three ways they're alike and ignore the 100 ways they're not.

3 ACTION: Once we have a mindset cemented, it dictates the action we take, don't take or let happen.

4 RESULTS: We then get results from that action which will be in line with our original thoughts.

5 | CAN-DO:
How to stop self-sabotage from negative mindsets

THE SELF-FULFILLING CIRCLE

Get results in line with thoughts
Poor score/place because "the greens are too fast"

Mindset drives:
What I do
What I don't do,
What I let happen

Tense over putts
Not much care over lining up
because...
   no point
   no belief
   no smooth stroke
   no follow through

4
RESULTS

3
ACTION

1
MINDSET

GETS
CEMENTED

2

Repeated thoughts become a mindset
"These greens are too fast"

Cherry-pick data/examples to show your mindset is right
One putt goes way past... "told you so"
Another putt is short... "so fast you dare not hit it"
Another putt goes in... "Luck! It would have gone miles past"

NEGATIVE MINDSET

Go round the **negative circle** for 'mindset on greens'.

Start with **1**. Repeated chat about the greens from their reputation or other players' experience is that "the greens are so fast they are almost impossible".

Now go round the circle and see how that **negative mindset drives negative results.**

5 | CAN-DO:
How to stop self-sabotage from negative mindsets

THE SELF-FULFILLING CIRCLE

Get results in line with thoughts
Great score/place because "these greens are just right for me"

Mindset drives:
What I do
What I don't do,
What I let happen

Look forward to the putts
Take care over lining up
   belief
   smooth stroke

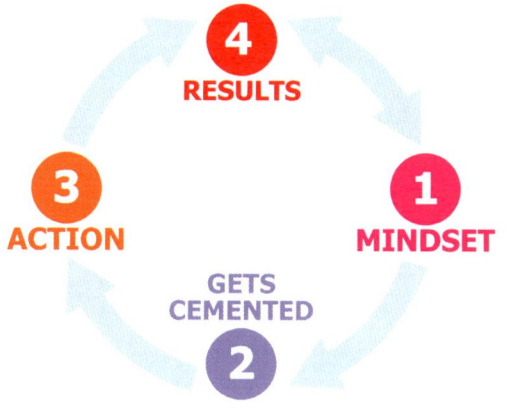

4 RESULTS

3 ACTION

GETS CEMENTED

1 MINDSET

2

Repeated thoughts become a mindset
"These greens are just right for me"

Cherry-pick data/examples to show your mindset is right
One putt goes way past... "shows the opportunity"
Another putt is short... "shows they are not too fast"
Another putt goes in... "Great! I've got it just right, and these greens can be an advantage for me"

POSITIVE MINDSET

- Now take a different **positive mindset** as the start point: "These greens are just right for me".

- Go round the circle, for the same situation as before and see how the **positive mindset drives positive results.**

MENTAL POSITION A versus **MENTAL BUNKERS**

MENTAL POSITION A

- I'm due for a birdie on this hole
- I'm the best in field at slow play
- He's so bad he needs them and more

MENTAL BUNKER

- I always mess up this hole
- Slow play makes me lose my rhythm
- I'm giving him too many shots

It's your **CHOICE** whether you use a **NEGATIVE MINDSET**, which is like playing from a **MENTAL BUNKER**. Or use a **POSITIVE MINDSET**. You can go further than just a positive mindset and go to **MENTAL POSITION 'A'.**

- Consider **TECHNICAL POSITION 'A'**: If you were allowed to place your ball anywhere within 100 yards of the pin, you would choose the very best spot; exactly how far from the pin, 60 yds, 85 yds? If pin on the left, place in the middle, left or right of fairway? On a slope or flat lie? In a spot settling down in the grass, or on a little tuft? You would continue to find the very best spot to the inch: POSITION A.

- You can't choose to play from technical position A, but you can choose to play from **MENTAL POSITION 'A'.** Do not accept just any positive mindset, but continue to improve it and improve it until you really have position A.

- Each time for any situation ask, **"What's Mental Position 'A'?" and choose it.**

- In every situation you can choose **Mental Position 'A'** and that will take you round the **+ve circle.**

TOOL SHEET: Mental Bunker Shots

TYPICAL LIMITING MINDSETS

Lessons don't work for me

It's fine on the practice ground, not on the course

Slow play destroys my rhythm

It's difficult to give 6 shots

If I start badly, the round's ruined

I've got a big slice today

I can't play if I've had to rush to the tee

The mental game doesn't apply to me

The greens are too...

The sand in the bunker is too...

I always mess up this hole

I'm no good at...

The pin positions are impossible

The people behind are rushing us

Mental games don't work because they can't fix a slice/hook/backswing

I'm fine on the mental game, my problem is a technical one

MENTAL POSTION 'A'

TOOL SHEET: Mental Bunker Shots

MY TYPICAL LIMITING MINDSETS (Mental Bunker)

ALTERNATIVE POWERFUL MINDSETS

(Mental Postion 'A')

TOOL SHEET: Tough Mental Bunker Shots

Just as technically there are normal bunker shots and **TOUGH BUNKER SHOTS**, so it is for mental bunkers. These two tool sheets will help you identify your deeper **limiting mindsets**, and help you take **MENTAL POSITION 'A'.** Write down what comes to mind in answer to these questions.

What I believe about me as a golfer:

What I believe others think of me as a golfer:

What I believe about golf (in relation to me):

From the above answers, those beliefs which most limit me are:

5 | CAN-DO:
How to play from Mental Position A

TOOL SHEET: Tough Mental Bunker Shots

Limiting belief (Mental Bunker)

Ways to doubt its truth (Create examples and evidence to the contrary: "It only takes one fly in the spaghetti to choose to send it all back")

New more powerful mindset (Free drop to mental position 'A')

Ways to support the new (Cherry pick data to support the new mindset; fabricate a little)

Climb the Ladder of Commitment
(on the new mindset)

repeat + repeat	write + repeat	tell + repeat	hear + repeat

"Think what you've always thought, you'll do what you've always done, you'll get what you've always got. If nothing changes... nothing changes".

"If what you believe were really true, there would be no need to believe it".

"A belief is choice, not chance, so change it".

SELECT CHAMPAGNE

REFUSE POISONED CHALICE

Mindsets often start by what other people say; and others agree with and repeat. You can even get a group limiting mindset.

- Don't accept other golfers' limiting thoughts. They are a **POISONED CHALICE**. Refuse them in your mind and **SELECT CHAMPAGNE** thoughts for yourself.

  - How do you take your coffee? Black, white, with or without sugar? If you were given coffee the way you dislike it, you'd not touch it. **Don't 'drink' other golfers' limiting thoughts.**

- **Example:** e.g., Playing partners complain about the slow play, and that it disrupts one's rhythm. Internally refuse this mindset. Choose instead "Slow play gives me an advantage because others get upset by it, and I can manage not to"

- Use the attached scorecard to note the poisoned chalices you manage to refuse, and the champagne you choose.

5 | CAN-DO:
How to stop being affected by others' attitudes

TOOL SHEET: Refuse poisoned chalices

Poisoned Chalice Refused (Mental Bunker)	Champagne Chosen (Mental Position 'A')

6 | RESULTS-DRIVEN
Want to score better, hit it better, or what?

PERFORMANCE TRIANGLE

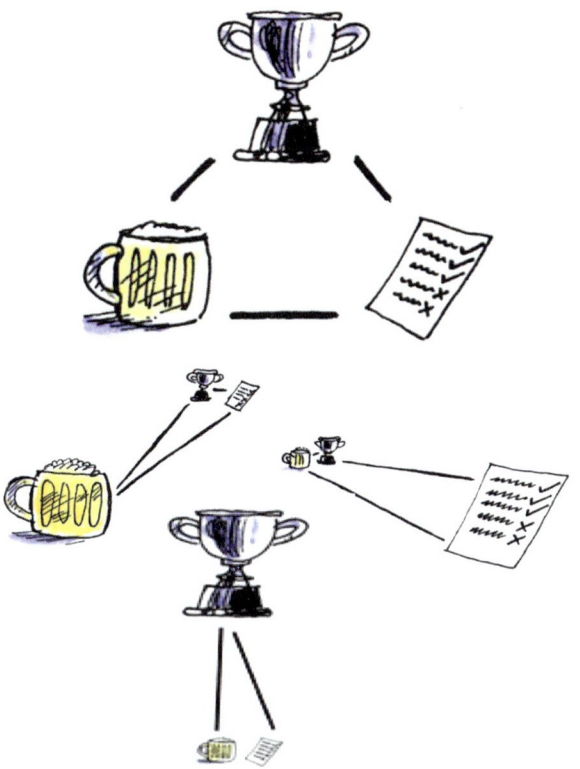

"Many people go fishing, but don't realize it's not the fish they're after"

- **Top performers** use a triangle to choose where they want to be in the 3 areas of
  (A) Achievement: (the score)
  (B) Enjoyment: (having fun) and
  (C) Learning: (doing it better)
  They choose a different balance for each different golfing activity..

- **Average performers** aren't clear exactly what mix of the 3 they want when playing or practising...

  e.g. trying out a new tip in competition and so don't score well, and end up frustrated; feeling a card is ruined so switch to having fun, and making the card worse; hitting balls on the range for fun, instead of practising chipping – then later getting upset on the course by fluffed chips.

ACTION: Decide the different balance you want from practice, social rounds and competition, and focus on that balance

6 | **RESULTS-DRIVEN**
How much better do you want to score?

77

A Small goals or STEPCHANGE goals

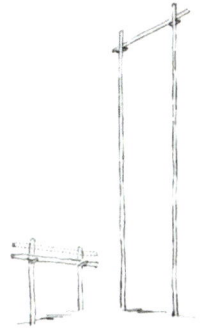

Pole vault

Ladder

Trampoline

Fly over

Cut down

B

HCP 19-18

- Play more
- Practise a little
- Take a lesson
- New tips
- Ignore non-technical

HCP 19-9

- Play less
- Practise a lot
- Take courses of lessons
- Get expert in distance reality
- Get expert in the 7 Thinking Techniques

Consider in section **A**, the system of **small goals** and the first bar on the left.

How do you know how high to set it? Ask yourself the question: "How high did I jump last time?" You set it there. Get over. Set it a little higher. Get over. This small goal system will only ever get you slightly better.

Consider in section **A**, the system of **STEPCHANGE goals** and the second bar on the right.

How might you get over that? Many different ideas come to mind on 'how to get high'. All of them will get you higher than the high jump method.
The **STEPCHANGE goal** helps you to change what you are doing.

Consider in section **B**, a 19hcp player who works during the week wants to get better. If the goal in their mind is to get to 18, one set of action steps occurs to them. But if they think of getting to a 9, a completely different set of action steps occurs to them. They may not get them to a 9, but they'll get them a lot lower handicap than the first set of ideas.

ACTION: Top performers use **STEPCHANGE goals** vs. **small goals** to get an improvement

Set yourself the target to save 5, 10 or 15 shots.

6 | RESULTS-DRIVEN
How much do you really want it?

First Law of Performance

Intentionality   **Techniques**

Result

The 1st Law of Performance is that the **Results** you get are a function of the **Intentionality you have** to achieve those results, and the **Techniques** you use.

Intentionality is key: it's the combination of determination, will, perseverance, grittiness. Remember:

'The man on top of the mountain didn't fall there'. 'No method will work unless you do'. Hannibal said "We will find a way, or we will make one" — that's **Intentionality.**

Intentionality can be built. Yet many golfers have low Intentionality on the improvements they seek, the round they are playing, and even on this shot. Consider an aim to improve scores by taking fewer putts:

Low Intentionality: May spend a short time on putting green, but then go to the range to hit balls; puts limits on what they'll do to putt better – won't want to change grip; and no need to change putter; they've putted well in the past with their current technique; may not even bother to count putts per round

High Intentionality: Will do what it takes to save those shots; take a lesson; test for 20-minutes each new grip, left hand down; claw grip; longer putter, shorter, heavier, lighter; seek and do practice drills from YouTube; learn to read greens. etc etc etc until you get the desired result.

ACTION: Use the following techniques to build intentionality on performance improvements, or on a round or shot.

6 | RESULTS-DRIVEN
How to build your determination to improve

Pull... A GOAL

Push... A GOAD

Pull & Push... GOAL & GOAD

Your **INTENTIONALITY** to carry something out is a combination of both the **PULL FORCES...** the pleasure of achieving the goal, and **PUSH FORCES...** the pain if you stay as you are.

Top performers use both... **goals and goads**

Average performers tend just to use goals... and that's not as powerful.

Example: God, to get people to follow the Ten Commandments, used not only gaining the pleasure of Heaven (a big **GOAL**) but also avoiding the pain of Hell (a big **GOAD**)

Example: Top sports people don't just want to win (**GOAL**); they learn to **HATE** to lose (**GOAD**)

The 'Improve Putting' Example: The **GOAL** is lower scores. But how could you also **GOAD** yourself with questions to make yourself dissatisfied with **NOT** improving your putting? For example: how stupid to get within 50 yards in 2 and then take 4 more! What a waste of time striking so well and then missing 5ft putts! How often do I get beaten by worse players just because they get lucky with putts, and I don't? How pathetic to keep messing things up on the green, when it's the easiest thing to fix?

LADDER OF COMMITMENT

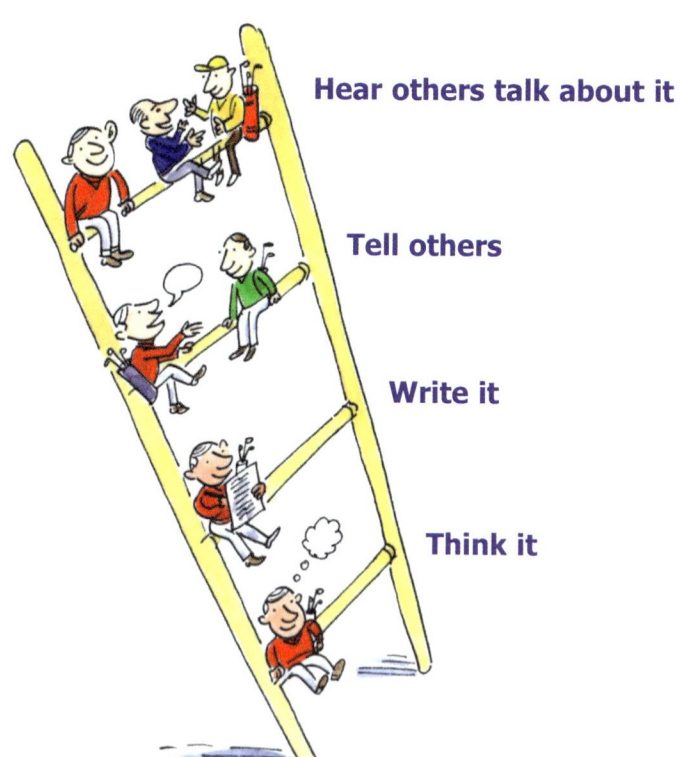

Hear others talk about it

Tell others

Write it

Think it

Are you now ready to use these techniques?

- **Write down** now, "I will become expert at 'X' technique"

- Print your name underneath. Sign it. Date it.

- **Tell others** you are becoming expert at "X" technique

- **Hear others talking** about the fact you are becoming expert at 'X' technique

As you do each of the steps above, you become more and more committed. It's called climbing the ladder of commitment, to increase your intentionality. If you just think it, as you are now doing, commitment is weak.

- **To increase your intentionality on any of your golf activities, climb the ladder of commitment.**

6 | RESULTS-DRIVEN
How to stop giving up a bit and instead hang-on

SECOND LAW OF PERFORMANCE

PERFORMANCE ZONE

RESULT

NO RESULT + A STORY

NON-PERFORMANCE ZONE

Story: Greg Louganis the American Olympic gold medalist diver talks about the sweet spot on a diving board. "When you hit it, you zoom up to the perfect position at the top, which makes a great dive easy. Some divers think therefore the secret of top performance is hitting the sweet spot. It's not. That's luck. The secret is what you do when you **don't** hit it... getting to the right place from the wrong place." It's the same with your mind: the secret is how to get to the right place from the wrong place.

- **The 2nd Universal Law of Performance** is that, after a performance, you end up in one of two zones: either with the **result** you wanted, or with **no result + a story.**

- Just listen to clubhouse conversations. With those who got the result they wanted the conversation is short: "How did you do?" – "Played to my handicap, thanks". With those who didn't: "How did you do?" triggers a long rambling story.

- The key is when you find yourself in the round 'concocting in your head the story you'll tell afterwards' – you have slipped from the **performance zone** to the **non-performance zone**. And you need to flip back to focusing on your result.

- For golf the secret is not to never slip into the **non-performance zone**, it is in realizing when you are beginning to concoct a story, and flipping back to the **performance zone** at once to focus on the **result** you now want, which is performance on the very next shot.

- Note that some people don't have to concoct a story during a round; they bring their story with them to the first tee. They don't even get on to the performance field. The same happens to their practice or their lessons.

6 | RESULTS-DRIVEN:
How to avoid 'more in hope than conviction'

UNTRY

'Do'

I'll try

...or 'Don't do'

- Are you now ready to try to put these techniques into action to improve your scores? That's **NOT** top performance.

- Do this test. **Please follow instructions exactly:** "**Try** to put your mobile phone on the floor". If it ends up on the floor you have done it; if it ends up anywhere else, you have not done it. Now **try** to do it. What was the result? You either did it or you didn't do it ...but there is no such thing as **try**.

- For most of our actions here is no such thing as trying. **"Trying is just a noisy way of not doing something".**

- At the STARTPOINT of any performance e.g. about to putt, about to learn a non-technical skill, there is no such thing as try. You have either got yourself to a state of being sure you will get the putt, or you haven't. Never say to your foursomes partner, "let me try to get mine in first". Either step up sure to get it in, or back off until you have got yourself sure.

- Take the word **'try'** out of your vocabulary. Poor performers "try harder". **Top performers 'untry'** their lives... they either 'do' or 'don't do'. They get themselves to a state of being sure they will do it, or they step away until they are. They never 'try' to do it.

7 | SELF-START
Get putt get confidence – or get confidence get putt?

- Where do feelings such as confidence come from?

- Can you buy confidence spray in a shop? No, feelings come from within. They come from your thoughts.
  They are self-generated.

- This is called **'self-start'** because it teaches you the thinking to self-start the moods you want (the confidence which gets you the putt) rather than wait for an **'outside-start'** (the putt that gives you confidence)

- It helps you **'self-start'** yourself (with the moods and feelings you want) rather than **'self-stop'** yourself (with the moods and feelings you don't want)

PLAY INSIDE OUT...

...versus OUTSIDE IN

CONFIDENCE SPRAY

ANXIETY CREAM

PRESSURE LOTION

FRUSTRATION OIL

7 | SELF-START
Get putt get confidence – or get confidence get putt?

PLAY INSIDE OUT versus OUTSIDE IN

Play Inside-Out

What happens

Play Outside-In

What happens

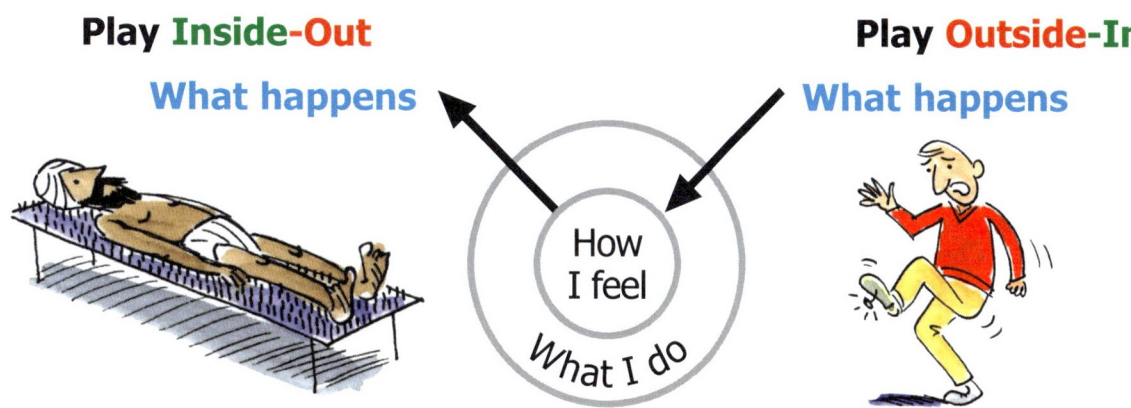

How
I feel

What I do

I happen to the world

The world happens to me

There are two models of playing:

- **Inside-Out**: I decide **how to feel**. That decides **what I do** which decides **what happens**.

- **Outside-In**: **What happens** decides **what I do** which decides **how I feel.**

- It's the difference between **'The World happens to me'** and **'I happen to the World'.**

- Think of the number of golfers and instances where they are playing outside in, rather than inside out.

- How does one play **Inside-Out**? **You must first decide how to feel.**

THREE LEVERS TO CHANGE YOUR MOOD

ANXIOUS   **FRUSTRATED**   **UNSURE**

CALM   **FOCUSED**   **CONFIDENT**

Peak performance states

There are 3 main moods you need for golf: a combination of Calm, Focused and Confident.

You can 'do' a mood or feeling easily. You have lots of practice:

- If the children are panicking, you 'do' calm. And you do it well enough to calm them down.

- If people are worried and unsure, you 'do' confident, often well enough to make them confident too.

You do it by the way you use **(1)** your **body**; **(2)** your **words** and their tone; **(3)** by what you **focus** on.

These are your 3 levers.

7 | SELF-START
How to stop being anxious, frustrated or unsure

THREE LEVERS TO CHANGE YOUR MOOD

Body   **Words**

A worLd behind each word

Focus

If you want to change your mood, change your

1 BODY: There is a real link between your mood and how you hold your body.

- Stand up and smile to the heavens. Try to be sad. You can't.
- Go into a slump, bored position. Try to be alert. You can't.
- What would happen if Monty skipped?

2 WORDS: There is a 'whole worLd behind each word'.

- Calling that hole a 'disaster' accesses one mood.
- Calling that hole a 'hiccup' accesses a different mood.
- Telling yourself you're 'excited' is different to telling yourself you're 'nervous'.

3 FOCUS: 'Two men looked out through prison bars. One saw mud, the other saw stars'.

- Focusing on mud makes one down and depressed
- Focusing on stars makes one up and optimistic

TOOL SHEET: Body Options

You can 'snap out' of any unwanted mood by making a snap change to your body e.g. 5 deep diaphragmatic breaths (breathe in with tummy out; breathe out with tummy in), run, trot, skip, splash water on head, face, loosen clothing, tighten clothing, tighten laces, touch toes six times etc.

What 'snap' body options will I use to snap out of an unwanted mood?

....

....

....

....

....

....

What are my body options to get into the 3 key desired moods?

Calm: e.g. • The Couples shoulder shrug
• 5 deep diaphragmatic breaths

....

....

....

Confident: e.g. • Woods' red shirt. Head up.

....

....

Focused: e.g. • Woods reading a putt with hands cupped by his visor

....

....

....

7 | SELF-START
How to stop being anxious, frustrated or unsure

TOOL SHEET: A worLd behind each word. A cranial website for each word

If I say the word 'meeting', the only way you know what is meant is to go to your own cranial website for meeting and finding your life experience of meetings e.g. too many, too long, too boring. If I say 'race meeting' you go to a different website and get completely different feelings. **Consider these examples and then complete your own list for golf.**

WORD	POSSIBLE ALTERNATIVE	MY TYPICAL WORD	POSSIBLE ALTERNATIVE
lazy	storing energy		
lonely	available		
oh shit!	oh poo!		
bunker/trap	sand		
giving shots	so bad he needs shots		
double bogey	rebound possibility		
hazard	recovery opportunity		
disaster	hiccup		
mess-up	blip		
terrible	below average		
awful	unusual		
lousy	not like me		
green in regulation	birdie putt		
bogey	one to even out		

THREE PEAK PERFORMANCE FEELINGS

- **The peak performance state** you want to be 'in the zone' is a combination of **confident, calm** and **focused**.

- Use your **body, words** and **focus** to get in these states.

- **Build three scrapbooks.** One which reminds you of occasions, in any sphere of life, in which you have felt very **confident**. The next: **calm**. And the third: **focused**. What could go in them?

- Imagine how you looked, how you felt, how you sounded when you were in each state.

- On the course, when you need to reinforce your mood, simply mentally go through the scrapbook in your mind. And aim to **look, sound** and **feel** as you did then.

TOOL SHEET: Scrapbooks – What I will remember to feel

Confident	Relaxed	Focused

What it felt, looked and sounded like on the above occasions:

7 | SELF-START
How to get your best moods, leave others behind

TRICKS OF THE TRADE

A

B

C

D

A Leave your twin behind

- Be on the train, face him on the platform. Offload all your bad, lousy thoughts and attitudes on to him
- Keep all the great ones to yourself...confident, calm, focused.
- Let yourself leave on the train gradually, waving goodbye, until he's out of sight; turn round and you are on your way to your round/next hole/next shot.

B Go peripheral

- Can't be tense when in peripheral vision. Consider high-speed police drivers, midfield player in football or rugby. Calm goes with seeing what's happening peripherally. Contrast with angry vision on just what's in front - you don't see the periphery. Cannot stay angry when you go into peripheral vision.

C Tai Chi it

- Combine with deep diaphragmatic breaths.
- Breathe in/pull in calm; breathe out/push out anxiety: in/pull confidence; out/push unsure; in/pull focused; out/push frustrated. Breath in/pull in good; breathe out/push out rubbish.
- On the course, do the breathing between shots, doing the Tai Chi in your head.

D Use mental triggers

- Like the first note of your favourite song, like a holiday photo or a certain smell brings feelings instantly. e.g. knuckle rap; high five; shaft twiddle; arm pump. What triggers do you have, or could you develop?

GET FRESH versus **STAY HEAVY**

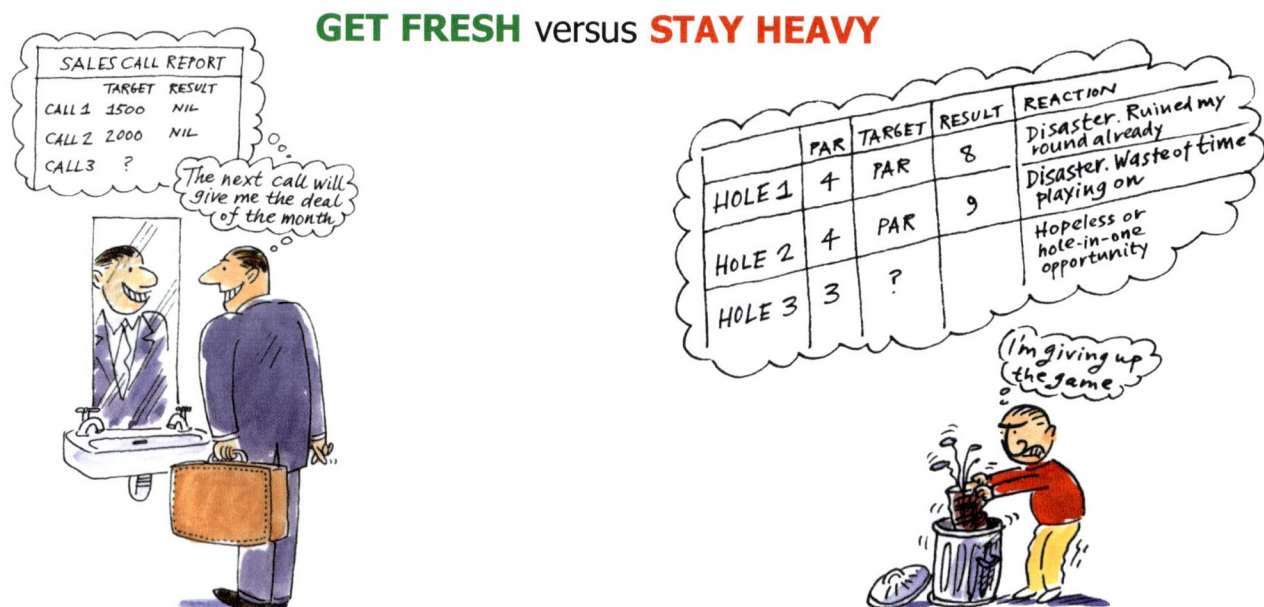

This thinking technique will illustrate two opposite feelings:

- **At work**, after two unproductive sales calls, he **freshens up** and makes the next call the best of the month.

- **In golf**, after starting with two bad holes, he **feels like giving up the game**, and doesn't realize the next hole is a hole-in-one opportunity.

Feeling A: HEAVY

Feeling B: FRESH!

Weighing on my mind

Exams over

Stone in my shoe

New job

Unfinished & nagging

Emigrating

- **Story:** Two monks had vowed never to touch a woman. One day they saw a beautiful girl trying to cross a stream. One monk bent down, picked her up, carried her over, put her down. They walked on in silence. After a time the second monk said: "Brother, we have vowed never to touch a woman. Why did you pick that woman up?" The first monk replied: "I put her down twenty minutes ago; why are you still carrying her?"

This illustrates the **HEAVY Feeling A**, of things weighing on your mind from what has happened, so you're not completely fresh. You are not good at the task you do at 11 o'clock, because of what happened in the meeting you had at 10 o'clock.

- Contrast this with the examples of **Freshness** of **Feeling B**. You are far more powerful for your next task if you can access **Feeling B**.

- So how do you get from **HEAVY Feeling A** to **FRESH Feeling B**?

FINISH UP and EMIGRATE

Do the the 1, 2 or 3 things

1..............................

2..............................

3..............................

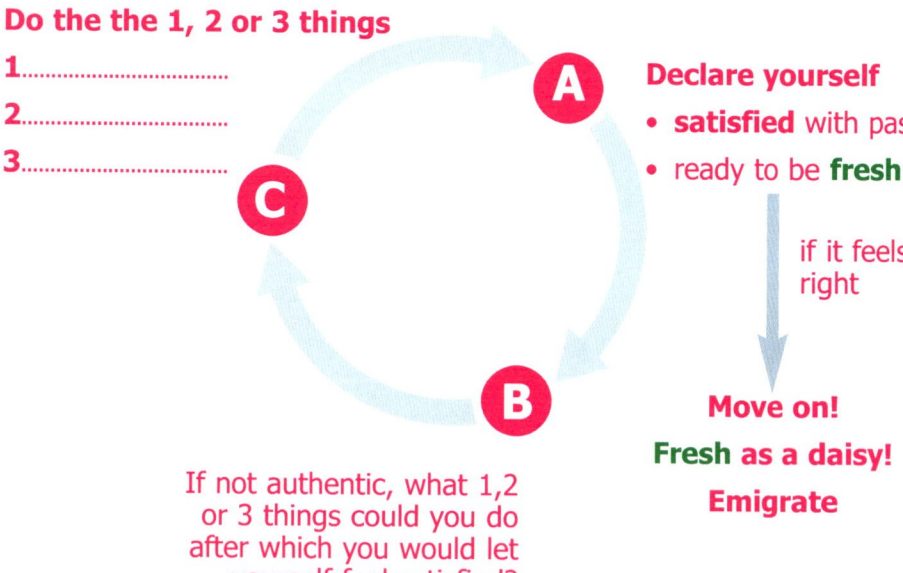

A **Declare yourself**
- **satisfied** with past
- ready to be **fresh**

if it feels right

Move on!
Fresh as a daisy!
Emigrate

B If not authentic, what 1,2 or 3 things could you do after which you would let yourself feel satisfied?

Create options!

Example: Consider firstly how you could move from the **'heavy'** feeling following a day at work, to be **'fresh'** for a great evening.

A Declare yourself satisfied with the day. "It's over, fine and I'm ready for a great evening".

B If that doesn't feel authentic, what 1, 2 or 3 things could you do before you could be able to feel satisfied? e.g. make a phone call; a note to yourself to do something tomorrow.

C Then do these things. Now satisfied? If so, go. If not, go round the circle one more time.

- Use also a physical trigger to **'put it all behind you'** e.g. punch the light switch, slam the door shut!

8 | FRESHEN-UP
How to stop previous events weighing on your mind

FINISH UP and EMIGRATE

Now apply this to your golf on the course. After a shot, a hole or an event, **'Finish-up and Emigrate'** to the next hole. Declare yourself **satisfied** and **fresh** for the next shot. If not authentic, what could you do, after which you'll feel satisfied and fresh? There will be two sorts of action you can combine:

A Mental resolutions (often to remedy the root cause of the mishap), e.g:

- decide to practice that shot for 30 minutes tomorrow
- decide never to take a driver on that hole again etc.
- decide to arrive 30 minutes earlier in future, so not rushed

B Physical triggers, e.g.
- untie and retie your shoelaces
- take out a new ball/glove
- empty left pocket into right and vice versa.

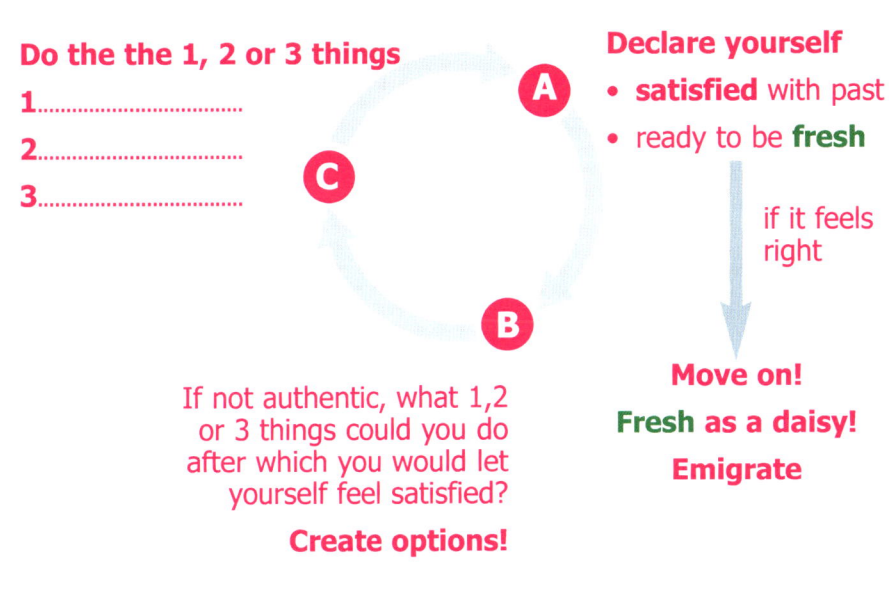

Do the the 1, 2 or 3 things

1...............................

2...............................

3...............................

C

A

B

Declare yourself
- **satisfied** with past
- ready to be **fresh**

if it feels right

Move on!

Fresh as a daisy!

Emigrate

If not authentic, what 1,2 or 3 things could you do after which you would let yourself feel satisfied?

Create options!

8 | FRESHEN-UP
How to stop a bad start ruining the round

TURN AT EACH HOLE, THEN AT EACH SHOT

Finish up at each hole: **Start** the remaining holes

- **Refresh** yourself on the 5th for the 'new 14' as much as you would at the 10th for the 'new nine'.

- **Refresh** yourself on the 15th for the 'new 4' as much as you did at the 10th for the 'new nine'.

- **Refresh** yourself on every hole as much as you do at the 10th... such that the 10th is no longer any different feeling.

- **Refresh yourself on every shot.**

- Most golfers only 'turn' after the first 9 holes. But many can then put the first 9 behind them and get ready for the fresh 9. They give themselves a **'10th tee feeling'**. If they have been doing badly they can 'turn over a new leaf' on the 10th tee. They are fresher on the 10th tee than they are on the 7th.

- Instead **'finish-up' on each hole**, and **get fresh** for the remaining ones i.e. give yourself that 10th tee feeling on each hole. Finish up and emigrate from the previous hole.

- **So on every tee:** "I'm finished with what's gone. I can give myself the 10th tee feeling. If not, what one or two things can I do, after which I can have the 10th tee feeling?"

- **So on every shot:** Finish up with the shots played so far and start your remaining shots now.

"The next shot is the first shot of the rest of my round".

9 | CLEAR-HEADED
Why 'Never-Up, Never-In' doesn't work

STOP SHORTIES: 1 Wrong Weight

We use a set of words to trigger a thought to trigger an action. But sometimes the words have been used so often, they become **tired and worn out**. They are just repeated from memory, and so don't actually trigger any thought so don't trigger any action.

Old Words: "Never up, Never In"

New Words: "How much have I missed the putt by?"

Question A: If you leave a 20ft putt short by 3ft, how much have you missed it by?

Answer: 5ft 11ins.

Why? Because you could gone past the hole by 2ft 11ins, and still be better off than 3ft short, for three reasons:

1 The putt had a chance of going in.

2 You will have seen the line back.

3 You are closer.

Question B: If you go past the pin by 3ft, how much have I really missed the putt by?

Answer: 1.5ft.

Why? Because ideal weight is to go through the hole by 1.5ft, so you've gone 1.5ft too far.

Clear-Headed Action: Count your 'TOTAL MISSED FOOTAGE' for each round you play.

9 | CLEAR-HEADED
Aim approach shots short, pin-high or beyond?

STOP ALL SHORTIES: 2 Wrong Aim

Beyond

Pin-High

Short

Aim approach shots short, pin-high or beyond?

Clear-Headed answer for a pro: It depends.

Clear-Headed answer for most **amateurs**: Always aim **BEYOND**, unless you MUST aim differently.

Why?: Golf courses are designed with most of the trouble at the front. For a central pin:

- If you aim beyond, and you hit it perfectly, there is no problem
- If you aim beyond, and mis-hit, you end up pin-high, and no problem
- If you aim at the pin, and mis-hit, you risk the trouble at the front
- If you aim to be short of the pin, and mis-hit, you'll likely miss the green

Powerful Mindset: problems with going beyond the pin are exaggerated, and for the amateur most times are less serious than being short:

- Nowadays you can get an accurate distance to the back, and so avoid risk of going over.
- The consequences of going over the back are anyway often low, and lower than being short. For each hole on the course have you really spent time examining exactly what's over the back? Have you dropped a ball and played from there? And then compared the risk of being there with being in trouble at the front?
- Downhill putts aren't an issue on most greens for amateurs, who anyway have trouble getting putts to the hole; and if you go past you'll have an uphill putt back, whose line you'll have seen.

CLEAR-HEADED ACTION: The concept of an 'APPROACH' shot is flawed. Hit a 'BEYOND' SHOT.

9 | CLEAR-HEADED
"Right club, just didn't catch it right?"

STOP ALL SHORTIES:
3 Wrong Club

The Biggest Failing in being **'clear-headed'** is not taking enough club and **'Coming up Short'.**

This happens because of muddle-headed mindsets:

- Haven't measured recently your average yardage for each club **...THE IGNORANCE FAULT**
- Clubbing for your best ever distance versus your nowadays average distance **...THE WISHFUL THINKING FAULT**
- Thinking you ought to "only need a…" **...The VANITY FAULT**
- Thinking you ought to be able to hit an 8 iron this far **...THE MACHO FAULT**
- Thinking afterwards "The club was right, I just didn't hit it right". But what you mean by hitting it right, is actually hitting it perfectly. And most times in life you don't do anything perfectly. And by insisting the club was right for that distance, you are destined to make the same mistake again **...THE REPEATED FAULT**
- Blaming the wind, instead of yourself for not assessing correctly a 1, 2 or 3 club wind **...THE NOT MY FAULT**

CLEAR-HEADED ACTION: Club for your average strike – to beyond the pin – and be happy to be long if it happens, since 'trouble' is at the front of greens more than the back.

The most clear-headed mindset is:

"What club can I take to be **sure** of getting somewhat past the pin?"

"With this club, can I 'see' it getting there?" If not change, until you are really sure it will get there.

9 CLEAR-HEADED

Is the hole like a stopping train up to the pin?

STOP ALL SHORTIES: 4 Wrong Mental Model

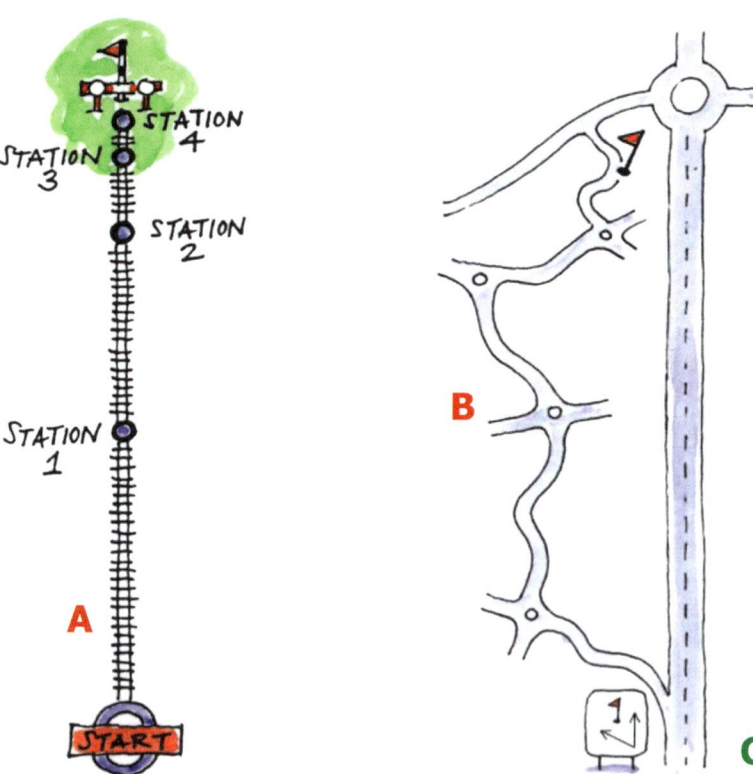

A Weak Mental Model

...treating the pin like the buffers at a railway terminus, which you 'approach' bit by bit, on a stopping train, getting ever closer.

B Weak Mental Model

...treating a hole like a car journey on side roads from tee to pin, left and right, stop and start, until you get there, 435-yards away.

C Strong Mental Model

...there's a motorway by the side of the fairway. Go up the motorway 450-yards to the roundabout, and come back 15-yards to the pin.

9 CLEAR-HEADED
Is the hole like adding coin after coin up to the pin?

STOP ALL SHORTIES: 4 Wrong Mental Model

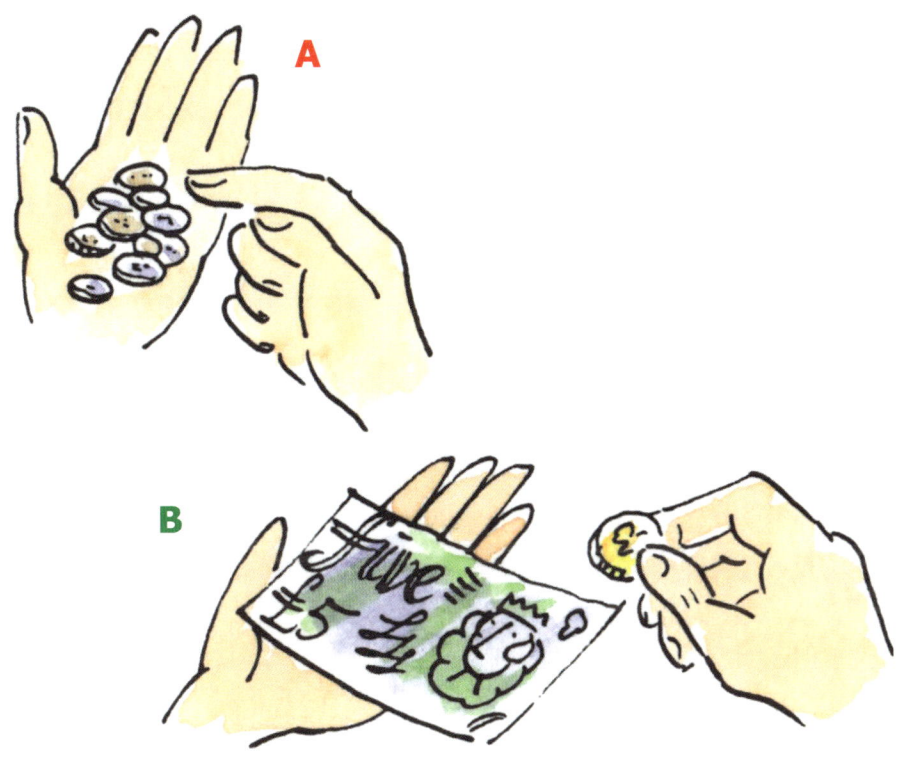

A

B

A Weak Mental Model

...like someone in the supermarket queue who spends ages adding one coin after another to get out the exact amount to get to the pin and no more.

B Stronger Mental Model

...is to pay with a note **...cover it and take the change.** Choose a club that will 'cover it' and get the putt back.

PRACTICE SCORECARD: GIVE UP SHORTIES

	Par	Score	To Pin	Chips/ Pitches	Missed Putts	Total Putts	Total 'S'
1			s 1 p	s 1 p	s 1 p		
2			s 1 p	s 1 p	s 1 p		
3			s 1 p	s 1 p	s 1 p		
4			s 1 p	s 1 p	s 1 p		
5			s 1 p	s 1 p	s 1 p		
6			s 1 p	s 1 p	s 1 p		
7			s 1 p	s 1 p	s 1 p		
8			s 1 p	s 1 p	s 1 p		
9			s 1 p	s 1 p	s 1 p		
OUT			s 1 p	s 1 p	s 1 p		
10			s 1 p	s 1 p	s 1 p		
11			s 1 p	s 1 p	s 1 p		
12			s 1 p	s 1 p	s 1 p		
13			s 1 p	s 1 p	s 1 p		
14			s 1 p	s 1 p	s 1 p		
15			s 1 p	s 1 p	s 1 p		
16			s 1 p	s 1 p	s 1 p		
17			s 1 p	s 1 p	s 1 p		
18			s 1 p	s 1 p	s 1 p		
IN			s 1 p	s 1 p	s 1 p		
TOTAL			1	1	1		

The CLEAR-HEADED WAY to save shots is to 'Give Up Shorties'

CLEAR-HEADED ACTION: Use the 'give up shorties' scorecard on the left. On any hole, once you are in range of the pin simply put a tick on the left of the little flag if your shot ends short (s) of pin-high; and a tick to the right of the little flag if your shot ends past (p). Then, the same for every shot thereafter, from your pitches and chips, right through to the putts. Count your shorties in a practice round. Aim to eliminate them; except for the **few** occasions you do it by deliberate intent.

Give Up Shorties, Save Shots

SHOT-SAVING PRACTICE:
Time with prime prospects

PRACTICE TIME

	Score Improvement potential %	Current %	Planned %
Driving	_____	_____	_____
Iron Play	_____	_____	_____
Chipping/Pitching	_____	_____	_____
Putting	_____	_____	_____
Non-Technical	_____	_____	_____
	100	100	100

AT WORK: You spend your time with the biggest sales opportunities, the biggest cost saving opportunities, the biggest profit opportunities. You don't spend time on small items just because you enjoy them or just because others are.

AT GOLF: Golfer after golfer 'mindlessly' hits balls on the range, because it seems fun and others are doing it – and ignore spending time on bigger and easier score improvement opportunities.

CLEAR-HEADED ACTION: apportion your practice time in line with where your score improvement possibilities are.

AT WORK: You ask for what you need to get a job done. If things aren't right, you don't sit back and complain, without making a specific suggestion for improvement.

AT GOLF: When things aren't right at a club, a golfer tends to moan, blame the committee, but not many make specific requests for bold change.

CLEAR-HEADED ACTION: Email NOW a SPECIFIC REQUEST for three practice facilities you need:

1 Request to **burn the 'No Chipping'** sign unless there's a chipping green. Even better, request to use the green to practice **'up and downing'.**

2 What's the point of new **distance finders** if we can't practice hitting each and every distance? Please set up physical targets at every **10 yards**, including under 100 yards.

2 Why do other sports have goal posts and we don't? Whenever ball fight matters, other sports use rugby-style posts to **practice through** and over. Please supply some.

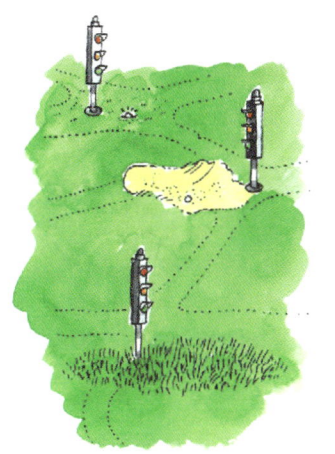

MUDDLE-HEADEDNESS: Many golfers know that one way to improve their scores is to improve their 'Course Management', but despite knowing it, it doesn't happen. Even when another suggests a better way to plot their way round the course, or a new way to play a hole better, the golfer doesn't take it on board.

THE REASON: Because the decision on what shot to play has other factors in it than just being 'Plotter Patrick' to find the safest way to get the lowest score. For example, part of me says: I want to see how far I can hit my driver; I'd like to try that shot over the water; I'd like to see if I can bend it; I don't want to take an iron off the tee; the round's ruined now anyway, so I might as well have a go with my XX club.

CLEAR-HEADEDNESS: What will work? It's not so much 'COURSE'-management that's needed as 'SELF'-management. We all have about 6 different 'SELVES' we can be. You need to decide who you are being as a golfer at any time, and who you want to be, and change. Are you being Steady Eddy; Adventurous Andy; Carefree Caroline; Not-serious Norman; Pathetic Patrick; or Clever Claudia? Choose who you want to be at any stage is the way you'll learn to shave the shots you can, or elect not to.

9 | CLEAR-HEADED
Favourite old clubs or low-scoring clubs?

1 Muddle-Headed: "There's nothing wrong with my clubs, it's me that's the problem".

Clear-Headed: Don't wait to change until there's something 'wrong'. Change because there are now lots of 'better' clubs, to get you lower scores. Just as there's nothing wrong with old TVs, computers, phones, cars, SatNavs, Internet speeds: just ones that are better.

2 Muddle-Headed: "If there's nothing wrong with them, it's not worth the money to change".

Clear-Headed: Don't be daft. Compare the cost of clubs with the money you'll spend on the game in the next few years. Compare the cost of clubs per hour of use with e.g. the cinema.

2 Muddle-Headed: "I know how to use these, and afraid I won't be able to use the new ones".

Clear-Headed: Manufacturers know that fear; that's why they make clubs easier to hit, with bigger sweet spots, friendlier shafts, better balance, different looks and feels, and you can try them out. E.g. why do they call clubs 'rescue clubs'? Because they are so much easier to hit!

CLEAR-HEADED ACTION: Get yourself the best driver for your swing; a 3 wood you can hit (for you) a long way; throw out all irons stronger than a 6; fill in the gaps with 3 rescue/hybrids: make sure your wedges have lofts evenly spaced; test out a load of new putters, including the long ones; get custom fitted if you can.

CLEAR-HEADED
What are your on-course triggers?

Current Triggers: A trigger is a reminder or stimulus on how you should think or play. To help their mood, some golfers have been known to wear a red shirt! Others have lucky mascot club covers. Others a lucky ball marker. But the use of on-course triggers is still very undeveloped. For example, in tennis to create a 'fresh start' many players untie and retie their shoelaces, tight. Golfers could too.

Ball Marker: What do you want to be reminded of as you prepare to putt? Get a marker with 'CAREER PUTT' on it to trigger yourself to focus on producing your best ever putt. Have another marked 'DAYTMTPYOTG' – standing for "Don't allow yourself to miss the putts you ought to get". Another saying, "17-INCHES THROUGH".

Tees: Each time you tee-up, you may be needing to collect yourself a little: you may have just marked a bad score on a hole, and you will likely have missed one of your last two putts. Why have a message on your tee-peg of the name of the golf club? Instead use it to trigger one of the NEW GOLF THINKING techniques, such as Spiral Up, or 10th tee feeling.

Short Tees: Hole-in-One Possibility.

Scorecard: Use the NEW GOLF THINKING scorecard to achieve best shot time after time, handle your score so far, avoid shorties, lower missed footage.

Ball: Mark it with a trigger: e.g. play a Titleist 'NOW'.

Distances on shafts: Put 3 labels on each wedge, noting the distance you hit each with 1/4, 1/2, and 3/4 swings.

CLEAR-HEADED
Who could best help you and why they can't

Who is the best person to give you a performance review?

Clear-Headed: Someone who:

A Sees me in action, and watches me make my score

B Can identify where I can best improve to get better results; and

C Can help me improve quickly in those areas.

Your standard swing teacher can't do this.

Who is the best coach for many handicaps?

Clear-Headed:

A A single-figure handicap player, who is good technically, and who likes to help others

B Who has also learned the 7 Thinking Techniques and can point me to them; and

C Who can be part of my playing group in competitions and observe me (e.g. in team events.) He can then give me tips, priority areas, and what to get further lessons on.

Why doesn't this happen?

Such a teacher would be so helpful he or she could charge a fee. They would be so popular they'd put many traditional teachers out of business. The Golf Authorities worldwide have banned this practice, by stopping any paid teacher playing in amateur golf events.

10 PUTTING IT ALL TOGETHER
How to use the Master Scorecard to get your best possible round

	3pt reason	Target for remaining holes	Focus on Career Shot mark improvers D, 9, 8, 7, etc	Score Pts	New target for round
					54pts
HOLE 1		BACK 18	54pts		
HOLE 2		BACK 17	51pts		
HOLE 3		BACK 16	48pts		
HOLE 4		BACK 15	45pts		
HOLE 5		BACK 14	42pts		
HOLE 6		BACK 13	39pts		
HOLE 7		BACK 12	36pts		
HOLE 8		BACK 11	33pts		
HOLE 9		BACK 10	30pts		
HOLE 10		BACK 9	27pts		
HOLE 11		BACK 8	24pts		
HOLE 12		BACK 7	21pts		
HOLE 13		BACK 6	18pts		
HOLE 14		BACK 5	15pts		
HOLE 15		BACK 4	12pts		
HOLE 16		BACK 3	9pts		
HOLE 17		BACK 2	6pts		
HOLE 18		BACK 1	3pts		

"I can get 3 Stableford points at each remaining hole, because each is either a par 3, par 5, a shot hole, or a short par 4."

You are now ready to use the NEW GOLF THINKING Master Scorecard (see next).

This incorporates several techniques in one and is the best way you can 'score' your round to help maximize your performance. The system comprises:

1 Step change Goals: Aim to get 3 Stableford points on each hole. People can imagine this because in the past they have got 3pts at all sorts of holes. Each and every hole is a potential 3 pointer because it is either a shot hole, a par 5, a par 3 or, for you, a short par 4. By contrast, gross scores are more difficult to imagine: e.g. "I've used most of my shots already and will have to play par golf form here" is difficult.

2 'Points on the Table' approach of snooker: Snooker players don't take the points they have so far and multiply that to imagine their final total. Instead, they look at 'the points still on the table' and don't give up whilst there are enough there. So in golf, after the first hole …there are still 51 'points on the table'.

3 Turn at each hole: Finish up. If you got 1 point on the first hole, 'Finish up and emigrate' to the 2nd hole, for the next 17. Get that '10th tee feeling'. The new target you can get for your round is 52pts. That's now the 'result' to focus on achieving. Focus on that result, no 'story'.

4 Best shot time after time: Within this overall strategy, now simply aim on each shot to do your 'career shot' with the full **RAF mental pre-shot routine**. And mark down all your Score Improvers. Ignore all other shots.

This has proven the most effective way of scoring, using several of your NEW GOLF THINKING techniques to really maximize your performance in a round.

10 | PUTTING IT ALL TOGETHER
The **New Golf Thinking** Master Scorecard

	3pt reason	Target for remaining holes		Focus on Career Shot mark improvers D, 9, 8, 7, etc	Score	Pts	New target for round
HOLE 1		BACK 18	54pts				**54pts**
HOLE 2		BACK 17	51pts				
HOLE 3		BACK 16	48pts				
HOLE 4		BACK 15	45pts				
HOLE 5		BACK 14	42pts				
HOLE 6		BACK 13	39pts				
HOLE 7		BACK 12	36pts				
HOLE 8		BACK 11	33pts				
HOLE 9		BACK 10	30pts				
HOLE 10		BACK 9	27pts				
HOLE 11		BACK 8	24pts				
HOLE 12		BACK 7	21pts				
HOLE 13		BACK 6	18pts				
HOLE 14		BACK 5	15pts				
HOLE 15		BACK 4	12pts				
HOLE 16		BACK 3	9pts				
HOLE 17		BACK 2	6pts				
HOLE 18		BACK 1	3pts				

The NGT Stop Slow Play Plan
CURRENT THINKING ISN'T WORKING

Nowadays, people are time-poor but rounds are taking longer. Frustration is increasing...

Yet committees feel they are doing their job...

by encouraging 'Avoid Slow Play At All Times'; re-issuing guidelines and tips on how to avoid slow play: issuing target times for the course and by hole... even though these actions are not solving the problem:

1 **Repeating Guidelines...** doesn't change ingrained, and almost sub-conscious, personal habits. The issue is not that golfers don't know what they should do: it is that they don't do it.

2 **Target Times by Hole...** are too complicated to work out and respond to whilst playing: and require playing group interaction, often difficult

3 **Penalties for Slow Play...** haven't worked: it's difficult to prove who is guilty; everyone always has an excuse; authorities don't want to upset a player, with a severe penalty, unfairly; difficult to be consistent.

An issue is that
"everyone has their own pet solution"

...along the lines of "if only others did this", e.g. 'They' should just:

- stop people marking cards on the green

- tell people to be ready to play when it's their turn

- stop people taking so long on their putts

- fix the known slow players, etc.

...So the need for new thinking isn't valued, since the perceived solution is for 'others' to implement the old pet thinking, which doesn't happen. The problem gets worse. New Thinking is needed.

THE SLOW PLAY SOLUTION

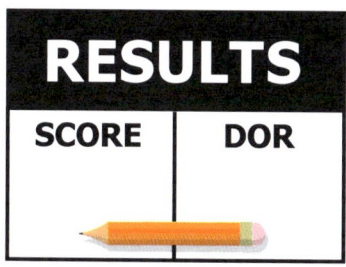

RESULTS

SCORE	DOR

1 BE RESULTS-DRIVEN on the KEY GOAL:

"A REDUCTION in DOR (duration of round) from X hrs to Y, by Z date."

2 TO IMPROVE DORs, IMPLEMEMENT NEW ACCOUNTABLE ACTION AT 3 LEVELS:

1 The INDIVIDUAL

2 The PLAYING GROUP

3 The LEADERSHIP

OLD THINKING...

Focuses on other things. It does not even measure, record nor communicate the key slow-play measure – your DOR. There is no real drive to improve this stat; neither a compelling goal (reward for good DOR), nor a meaningful goad (consequence for bad DOR).

NEW GOLF THINKING...

Focuses on DOR. Individual results (DOR) are measured, recorded and published for each round; and also average cumulatively for the season; displayed in rank order; and players classified in 3 categories as for playing handicap.

A CLUB QUIZ: 20 QUESTIONS TO CREATE NEW THINKING

1   How are slow players like meetings?

2   Why is slow play like "never-up, never-in"?

3   Why is slow play like how good a (car) driver you are?

4   How is slow play like junk emails at work?

5   How is slow play like bad breath?

6   Why is slow play like putting on your clothes?

7   Why are your slow play habits like a baby?

8   What does a video of your swing do that stop slow play efforts do not?

9   What do X Factor and Masterchef do that stop slow play efforts do not?

10 How should golfers be like survivors put in a lifeboat?

11 Which action helps most:
    A 'Not marking card on the green' or
    B 'Always catching up with the group in front'?

12 What is the key difference between the above actions **A** and **B**?

13 What are the 2 keys to high-performing groups?

14 What can a FedEx parcel or Amazon order teach stop slow play?

15 What can statues teach us about stop slow play efforts?

16 What can stop slow play efforts learn from Head & Shoulders?

17 How is pace of play unlike every other golf stat?

18 Why does a SatNav work, and the leadership's stop slow play efforts don't?

19 What can stop slow play efforts learn from bankers?

20 Why are some slow players like horse and water?

The answers can be found in three groups on the following pages...

A the individual
B playing group
C leadership

QUIZ ANSWERS A: NEW THINKING FOR EACH INDIVIDUAL

1 **How are slow players like meetings?** Take forever, we all moan about them, but don't change them.

2 **Why is slow play like 'never-up, never-in?'** Because talk about slow play is so hackneyed and clichéd it doesn't generate any new action. We just repeat the same-old, same-old.

3 **Why is slow play like how good a car driver you are?** Most people think they're above average at driving a car. But by definition, most can't be. In the same way, most people think they're above average at pace of play, and don't need to change at all; but by definition, most are only average and could do better

4 **How is slow play like junk emails?** Everyone gets junk emails – but no-one admits to sending any. Everyone sees others causing slow play, but don't think they do it themselves.

5 **How is slow play like bad breath?** If you've bad breath, nobody tells you to your face, just talk about you behind your back. The same with a slow player.

6 **Why is slow play like putting on your clothes?** Dressing involves habits you are not aware of: Which shoe do you put on first? Which sleeve? The same with their slow play habits – they are not aware of them.

7 **Why are pace of play habits like a baby?** You don't expect anyone to criticize your baby, nor your pace of play habits. But ask, "Can I tell you if the baby's ugly?" – and then tell them.

8 **What does video of your swing do that stop slow play efforts don't do?** The video shows you where you're going wrong, and can improve. Current stop slow play efforts don't **SHOW** or **TELL** any individual where they can improve.

9 **What do X Factor and Master Chef do that stop slow play efforts don't do?** All talent shows give feedback to an individual: how good or bad was their performance, and how could they do better next time. Traditional stop slow play efforts don't do this. **THIS IS THE SINGLE BIGGEST CHANGE TO MAKE.**

NEW GOLF THINKING: Individuals agree to give/take feedback on their slow-play habits

KEY NEW ACTION: Creative, periodic use of the SmartPlay Scorecard (next).

SMARTPLAY SCORECARD (WALK)

NAME: _____ **DATE:** _____

Mark ticks & crosses for instances of good & bad habits by your partner as you see them during the round

	✓ or ✗	Score 1-10
1 Shows attitude "Right place is just behind group in front" NOT "Just ahead of the group behind"		
2 When behind, plays when ready, even if out of turn, and encourages others to do the same		
3 Walks briskly between shots		
4 If first to play, is first to their ball.		
5 Prepares own shot whilst others are playing e.g. check distance, choose club, line of putt		
6 Gets line of sight on own ball, and others; has provisional handy, and plays one if in doubt		
7 Glove on; tee, ball, and club ready when turn on tee		
8 Marks card only whilst 'waiting'		
9 Leaves bag at exit to green		
10 Asks to putt out when feel they can		

Marker's signature

Player's signature

Sign, tear off & hand-in

Score out of 100

STOP SLOW PLAY – Five Insights

- It's like bad breath: we talk about it behind their backs, but don't help solve their problem.

- Slow play is due to habits we don't know we have; and attitudes we've never thought about.

- Slow play is always someone else's fault.

- This gives you a rare chance to help another player, yourself, and the field. Score honestly. "Can I tell you if the baby's ugly?" The answer for today is "Yes, please."

- Most golfers have unconscious bad habits. Some more than others. But most will want to correct them, if they are pointed out. Just like they want to learn and correct technical faults.

Find creative ways to use this scorecard: Get suggestions on a different top 10 faults; **or different priority order.** Ask to mark strongest 2 skills and 2 weakest. **Collect cards & publish 2 strongest, 2 weakest.** Give marks out of 10 on all 10.

The NGT Stop Slow Play Plan SMARTPLAY SCORECARD (CART)

NAME: _____ **DATE:** _____

Mark ticks & crosses for instances of good & bad habits by your partner as you see them during the round

	✔ or ✗	Score 1-10
1 Shows attitude "Right place is just behind group in front" NOT "Just ahead of the group behind"		
2 When behind, plays when ready, even if out of turn, and encourages others to do the same		
3 Uses a buddy system with the cart: drop off at one ball with enough clubs and go at once to the other ball		
4 If cart-path only always takes enough clubs with them		
5 Prepares own shot whilst others are playing e.g. check distance, choose club, line of putt		
6 Gets line of sight front & behind on own ball, and others; has provisional handy, and plays one if in doubt		
7 Glove on; tee, ball, & club ready when turn on tee		
8 Drives away before putting club away		
9 Leaves cart at exit to green		
10 Marks card only whilst 'waiting'		

Marker's signature

Player's signature

Sign, tear off & hand-in

Score out of 100

STOP SLOW PLAY – Five Insights

- It's like bad breath: we talk about it behind their backs, but don't help solve their problem.

- Slow play is due to habits we don't know we have; and attitudes we've never thought about.

- Slow play is always someone else's fault.

- This gives you a rare chance to help another player, yourself, and the field. Score honestly. "Can I tell you if the baby's ugly?" The answer for today is "Yes, please."

- Most golfers have unconscious bad habits. Some more than others. But most will want to correct them, if they are pointed out. Just like they want to learn and correct technical faults.

Find creative ways to use this scorecard: Get suggestions on a different top 10 faults; **or different priority order.** Ask to mark strongest 2 skills and 2 weakest. **Collect cards & publish 2 strongest, 2 weakest.** Give marks out of 10 on all 10.

QUIZ ANSWERS B: NEW THINKING FOR THE PLAYING GROUP

10 How should golfers be like survivors put in a lifeboat?

They are thrown together in a group, with no formal leader, but have to work together to survive; the same is true for a golf playing group needing to keep a good pace of play.

11 Which action helps pace of play most: A 'Not marking card on the green' or B 'Always catching up with the group in front?'

The second guideline is the biggest time saver of all actions

12 What is the key difference between the above actions A and B?

The first can be done by an individual; the second, the most valuable action of all, requires successful interaction within the playing group.

13 What are the 2 keys to high-performing groups?

A Common goal

B Each individual exercises their responsibility to influence the others to help achieve the result.

14 What can 'pace of play efforts' learn from a FedEx parcel or Amazon order?

You can easily track the progress of a FedEx parcel or Amazon order, but you can't easily track progress against a target pace of play (e.g. 2hrs 44mins to here).

NEW GOLF THINKING:
Declare each individual has a responsibility to influence the playing group

KEY NEW ACTION:
Institute a new 'NGT Group Etiquette

1 Initiate First Tee Preview

Playing group agrees their joint goals below.

Discuss what to do if get behind; ok to suggest to play ready golf; ok to tell me if I can improve on SmartPlay. If get miles behind, agree to play Catch-Up golf.

2 Agree Joint Goals

A Joint Goal: 4/4 In-Position Points

An easy measure: if we are in position, at each par 3, all our group will be on the tee, before the group in front has finished putting out. Usually, that gives 4 checkpoints. We will aim to achieve 4 out of 4.

B Joint Goal: Low DOR (Duration of round)

Agree to record DOR. Recognize new etiquette whereby each individual scores the DOR of the group, because each golfer has a responsibility to influence the pace of the group.

3 Each Tee Review

THE PROBLEM: difficult to calculate on any tee, how far ahead or behind one is versus target timing for that tee.

NEW GOLF THINKING: Attach a cheap timepiece to each tee marker; set each timepiece slow by the time it should have taken to that tee. E.g. if target 2 hrs 40 minutes to the 13th tee, set that timepiece slow by that much. The playing group notes their start time e.g. 11.29. Then at each subsequent tee if the timepiece shows a time later than 11.29, they are behind. The very presence of the timepiece triggers a quick each tee review.

ALTERNATE SOLUTION: Instead of designating times to tees, simply put markers where play should be after 1 hour, 2 hour, 3 hour, or even more frequent posts. Have different markers for 4-ball, 3-ball, 2-ball. passing the markers triggers the group review.

The NGT Stop Slow Play Plan
NGT 'CATCH-UP PACE' GOLF

On 1st Tee:

Agree to play Catch-Up Pace Golf when needed, or even from the start

Establish rapport with group ahead: will be right behind, but that's not over pushing; will not have hands on hips; will hit if can't reach; will raise club to ask if unsure. Establish rapport with group behind: we aim not to be slow; do hit if can't reach.

On tee:

No-honour – whoever is ready goes, and encourages others to be ready after.

Shorter hitters go first as soon as players in front are out of range.

Par 3's whoever can't reach, goes.

On fairway:

No group movement from ball to ball; each player at once to own ball, prepares their shot.

Walk forward to the level of own ball, even if far ahead, keeping if necessary to the side.

Go if ready, and not hurting others.

Go if can't reach.

Don't overreact to a ball rolling close on a shot behind.

On green:

Encourage players behind to play if can't reach green.

Putt out if you can.

If needed, first two finished leave partners and go drive off on next tee.

Always: have second ball in pocket, and play provisional if in doubt.

If ball lost, others leave the search to play their shot, one at a time, before rejoining search.

QUIZ ANSWERS C: NEW THINKING FOR THE LEADERSHIP

15 What can statues teach us about stop slow play efforts? Whoever heard of a statue erected to a Committee? Most successful projects have a leader. If they don't get results, get a new project leader.

16 What can stop slow play efforts learn from Head & Shoulders? H & S fixed your dandruff problem, but didn't offer aspirational hair. Once it added this, it became the worlds biggest shampoo. Similarly, current slow play efforts aim to get rid of the problem, but don't offer an aspirational state to get to: what's the opposite of slow play? Fast Play? That's not an aspiration: "I don't want to rush round, nor be hurried on my shots". The solution: redefine the aspiration, not as fast play, but as SmartPlay. People will want that, and won't want to be 'unsmart'.

17 How is pace of play unlike every other golf stat? Stats are published for everything, except the most important stat after your score: how long your round took (DOR-Duration of Round). And the time of your round is the time of your group.

18 Why does a SatNav work, and the leadership's stop slow play efforts don't? A SatNav works because it knows two things: where it starts from, and where it's going. Leadership of Slow Play efforts don't know the facts on current actual DORs, nor exactly where they want DORs to get to, by when.

19 What can stop slow play efforts learn from bankers? Bankers have been driven by bonuses promised by their leaders. Up to now there have been no bonuses for avoiding slow play: no bonuses for smart play (and l\ittle consequence if you're slow).

20 Why are some slow players like horse and water? You think the answer is you can take a horse to water but you can't make it drink. Well you can. Just put salt in its oats. The same way you can fix slow players. But if they resist playing smartly, there must be a consequence.

NEW GOLF THINKING:

Leaders commit to a DOR goal, then MEASURE, PUBLISH, FEEDBACK and REWARD IT.

KEY NEW ACTION:

Leaders declare the '10-point NGT Action Plan'.

The NGT Stop Slow Play Plan
LEADERSHIP RESPONSIBILITY: 10 MANDATORY NEW ACTIONS

1 COMMIT TO A COMPELLING DOR GOAL: e.g. 30-minutes off average DOR within 3 months.

2 ASSIGN A PROJECT LEADER: replace if fails.

3 DECLARE A MEASUREMENT SYSTEM:

- DOR (Duration of Round). Measured for the group from first drive to pin back on 18th.
- Noted on scorecards by players themselves, rely on honesty like score.
- An individual scores the DOR of group, recognizing the responsibility to influence the group.
- Over time, fast players will have cumulative lower DORs, slow players higher.

4 PUBLISH: all DORs, and cumulative DORs for each player, in league table order.

5 CLASSIFY: as for handicaps, designate 3 categories: Smart / So-So / Slow Players.

6 REWARD: decide 'ties' not by convention of count-back, but by order of DOR; announce 'Back of the field' policy for those who wish to play slow.

7 Creatively introduce IN-POSITION BONUS POINT Competitions. (A bonus point is given for each par 3 arrival, with group ahead still on green.) Track, publish and reward individuals bonus points.

8 Creatively introduce SMARTPLAY SCORECARD MARKING (e.g. start on Captain's Day; publish individual scores, or club collective, keep as personal feedback).

9 Creatively introduce CATCH-UP PACE GOLF days (e.g. institute it for the course one day a week, or a morning; or in a social competition.)

10 Supply SMARTPLAY FEEDBACK TIME-PIECES on each tee; or SMARTPLAY HOURLY MARKER POSTS.

THE ONE THING TO DO TO STOP THE PROs SO-SLOW PLAY

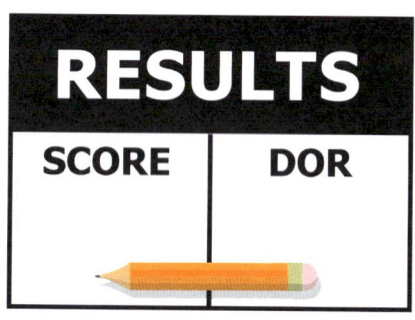

RESULTS

SCORE	DOR

'MEASURE, PUBLISH AND REWARD DORs'

At each Professional Tournament, 95% of the players end up in a tied position.

Current Thinking: Pros' prize money is split equally amongst those tied. This is only a convention – amateur ties have historically always been separated (by count-back, though ideally from now on by DOR).

New Golf Thinking: Either **A:** change the pros' convention and separate and reward tied pros by order of average DOR for the tournament; or **B:** give a bonus to the player amongst each set of ties who has the lowest DOR.

The Effect: Most of the field is involved in competing for DOR bonus money.

How Funded: Either redistribution of prize money from current sponsors.

Or, seek a DOR sponsor for extra DOR money; a sponsor who wants to be associated with stopping slow play; or a sponsor associated with speed of service or delivery.

Printed in Great Britain
by Amazon.co.uk, Ltd.,
Marston Gate.